FROM PERSIA TO NAPA
WINE AT THE PERSIAN TABLE

NAJMIEH BATMANGLIJ

WITH

Wine and Persian Poetry
Dick Davis

Pairing Wine with Persian Food
Burke Owens

MAGE PUBLISHERS
WASHINGTON, DC
2006

LIBRARY OF CONGRESS CATALOGING-IN-PUBLICATION DATA

BATMANGLIJ, NAJMIEH
FROM PERSIA TO NAPA : WINE AT THE PERSIAN TABLE / NAJMIEH BATMANGLIJ ;
WINE AND PERSIAN POETRY [BY] DICK DAVIS ;
PAIRING WINE WITH PERSIAN FOOD [BY] BURKE OWENS.
P. CM.
INCLUDES INDEX.
ISBN 1-933823-00-3 (HARDCOVER : ALK. PAPER)
1. COOKERY, IRANIAN. 2. IRAN--SOCIAL LIFE AND CUSTOMS. 3. WINE AND WINE MAKING.
I. DAVIS, DICK, 1945- II. OWENS, BURKE. III. TITLE.
TX725.I7B365 2006
641.5955--DC22

2006003666

FIRST HARDCOVER EDITION
ISBN 1-933823-00-3

PRINTED AND MANUFACTURED IN KOREA

MAGE BOOKS ARE AVAILABLE AT BOOKSTORES,
THROUGH THE INTERNET
OR DIRECTLY FROM THE PUBLISHER:
MAGE PUBLISHERS, 1032-29TH STREET, NW, WASHINGTON, DC 20007
202-342-1642 • AS@MAGE.COM • 800-962-0922
VISIT MAGE ONLINE AT
WWW.MAGE.COM

To the Persian poets,
with admiration and gratitude.

With wine beside a gently flowing brook – this is best;
Withdrawn from sorrow in some quiet nook – this is best;
Our life is like a flower's that blooms for ten short days,
Bright laughing lips, a friendly, fresh-faced look – this is best.

Hafez/Davis

با می بکنار جوی می باید بود

وز غصه کنارہ جوی می باید بود

این مدّت عمر ما چو گل دہ روز است

خندان لب و تازہ روی می باید بود

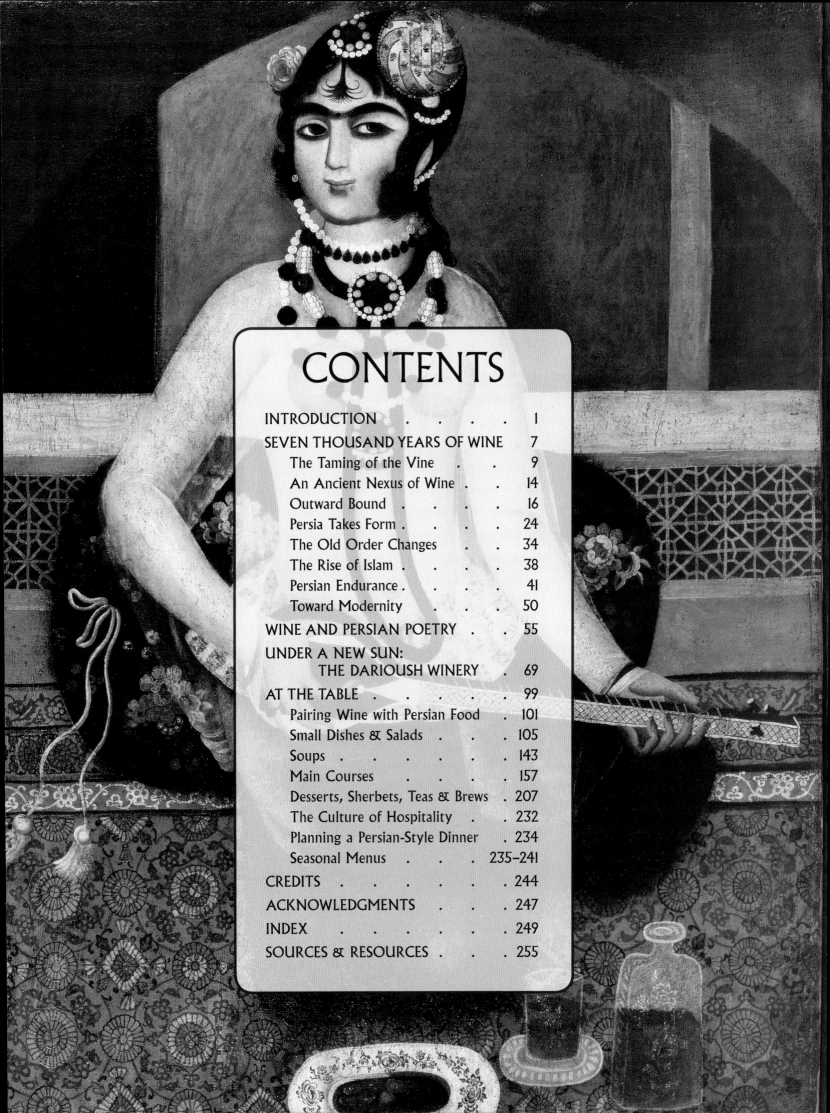

CONTENTS

INTRODUCTION

That's a question I have often been asked by colleagues in the culinary world and students in my cooking classes. The answer is surprising. It is also complex.

For thirteen centuries, the dominant religion in Iran has been Islam, which forbids the making, selling or drinking of alcoholic beverages. But the Qur'an—the holy book of Islam—isn't entirely consistent about this matter, and the strictness of the proscription has varied greatly over time. Even today, under a theocratic government, wine is drunk in many Iranian homes as a private pleasure. Some of it is made locally, although the vintners and wine merchants are non-Muslims. The present situation in the country is not unlike that of the United States during Prohibition, when a constitutional amendment banning alcoholic beverages was widely but cautiously ignored.

I grew up in Tehran in a traditional household. Whenever I get up early in the morning, I remember my father's gentle predawn whisper: "It's time to pray." Eating and drinking ceremonies figure in my most vivid childhood memories, but alcoholic beverages were not a part of them. Our drinks were tea and sherbets.

It was different at my aunt's house, however. Every afternoon around five o'clock, she would prepare a table in a shady spot in the garden. There, *noghl-e mey*—a term used since ancient times in Iran to refer to small dishes of sweets, savories and fruits that accompanied wine drinking—would be displayed and wine would be brought out for her husband and his friends. Just as we had afternoon tea ceremonies at our house, my uncle had his wine ceremony. It was his medicine, my mother would say.

When I was eighteen, I came to the United States for university studies. I continued to pray three times a day in the privacy of my own room. During those undergraduate and graduate school years, I had many friends from various backgrounds, and all were interested in Persian culture. Most had heard of Omar Khayyam—a brilliant twelfth-century astronomer and mathematician as well as a poet—and they usually could quote a snippet or two from the Edward FitzGerald translation of his *Rubaiyat*:

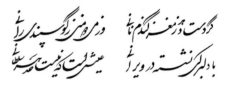

A book of Verse underneath the Bough,
A Jug of Wine, a Loaf of Bread—and Thou
Beside me singing in the Wilderness
O Wilderness were Paradise enow!

Shah Abbas, greatest of the Safavid Dynasty kings, receives wine from a saqi (wine server) in his harem in a seventeenth-century mural.

I explained to my friends that wine drinking was a frequent theme of Persian verse in that era, seen as a source of solace for the difficulties of this world and a means of apprehending the next.

For me, though, wine was still only an abstraction, since I didn't drink, not even a beer. That changed after I returned to Iran and married. My husband, Mohammad, was a wine enthusiast, and when we received a gift of some fine champagne from American friends, he persuaded me to try it. Thus I had a rather splendid introduction to wine: My first taste was vintage Taittinger Blanc de Blanc. Later, as post-Revolution refugees in the south of France, we made our own wine—Château Zal we called it, Zal being our first son, whose feet we used for pressing the grapes, the traditional method in France.

In the years since then, I have written extensively about Persian cuisine, one of the world's oldest cooking traditions. (The word "Persian" in English comes from the name of the province of Pars—also called Fars—in southwestern Iran, which was the center of the first Persian empire. In a cultural context, it is used interchangeably with "Iranian," derived from "Aryan," an ancient term for the Indo-European languages spoken by tribes in the region.) This part of the world played a key role in shaping other cuisines. It lay midway along trading routes, collectively known as the Silk Road, that linked Asia and Europe in ancient and medieval times. In addition to the back-and-forth traffic of trade goods, the routes served as conduits for the exchange of ideas, tastes and customs, including those related to eating and drinking.

The Near East was also where the domestication of the grapevine occurred, although that happened long before the Silk Road existed. Its cultivation spread in all directions from there, finding great favor in the land that would be home to the Persians. The fruit of the vine continues to hold a prominent place in Persian cuisine. A combination of grapes, bread and cheese was a full meal for many working Iranians during my childhood. Fresh grapes are eaten before meals and afterward, and fresh grape juice is a popular drink. Some grapes are dried to produce raisins. Unripe grapes *(ghureh)*, the juice *(ab ghureh)* and the reduced juice *(rob-e ghureh)* are all used as souring agents. Grape molasses *(shireh-ye angur)*, produced by boiling down grape juice, serves as a sweetener (it was used before sugar was known). In all, hundreds of varieties of grapes are grown in Iran at present—cultivated in practically every part of the country except along the hot southern coast. Yet wine, regarded in many cultures as the supreme gift of the vine, is proscribed.

How, then, should wine drinking be viewed by all those who cherish the pleasures of the Persian table? My answers will take us far back in time, all the way to the dawn of human civilization (for a quick guide, see the map on pages 14–15). We will travel across vast spaces, venturing as far afield as the Napa Valley in

California (pages 69–97), where an Iranian-American named Darioush Khaledi is honoring his heritage at a state-of-the-art winery, whose architecture is inspired by the ancient Persian capital of Persepolis. Along the way, Dick Davis, a leading authority on Persian literature, will discuss the theme of wine drinking in Persian poetry (pages 55–67). And Burke Owens, an expert on wine-food pairings and the associate curator of wine at COPIA (a museum and cultural center for wine, food and the arts in Napa), will offer guidelines for matching various wines with Persian dishes (pages 101–103). Finally, I have created 80 recipes—for small dishes and salads, soups, main courses, desserts, sherbets, teas and brews—that you might choose for the partnerings. Suggested menus appear on pages 235–241, but the possibilities are truly endless.

I hope you will enjoy the journey and all that it can lead to.

Inscribed around the rim of this agate wine cup is a poem mentioning Jamshid, a legendary Iranian king whose many gifts to humankind included wine:

> *This cup, which gives good news of rose-colored*
> *Wine, is [worth] more than a thousand of Jamshid's goblets.*
> *When it is filled with rosy wine, you would say it is*
> *A cloud lit by the brilliance of the sun.*

The cup belonged to a fifteenth-century ruler, Sultan Husayn, seen holding it at right, with his harem dancing below a palace balcony.

SEVEN THOUSAND
YEARS OF WINE

Fashioned by silversmiths of the Proto-Elamite culture around 3000 B.C.E., a six-inch-high kneeling bull holds a spouted vessel that may have been used for wine libations. The Proto-Elamites, centered in southwestern Iran, often represented animals in human postures in their art.

On the opposite page, a bird-shaped vessel from Uruk in Mesopotamia (circa 3300 B.C.E.) and a cluster of Shiraz grapes (grown in Napa, California) are shown.

"Whoever seeks the origins of wine must be crazy," a Persian poet once wrote, implying that such a quest is not only hopeless but also irrelevant: Enjoyment is what matters.

Certainly winemaking has always been tinged with mystery. Just how the juice of grapes can become wine wasn't understood until the mid-nineteenth century, when the French chemist Louis Pasteur showed that microscopic single-celled plants called yeasts consume the sugar in the liquid and turn it into carbon dioxide and alcohol. Even today, when technology allows tight control over fermentation and other phases of winemaking, achieving excellence is a kind of art, with success depending on chemical processes of baffling intricacy.

As for the beginnings of viniculture—a term that embraces both the growing of grapes and making of wine—uncertainties abound, although it is clear that the first steps were taken very long ago, at a time when humans began to give up the nomadic hunter-gatherer lifestyle that had sustained them for several million years. This first happened around 8000 B.C.E. along the northern fringe of the Fertile Crescent in the Near East. In the cool uplands there—the plateau country of eastern Turkey, the area known as Transcaucasia between the Black and Caspian Seas, and the Zagros foothills of northwestern Iran—humans pioneered a radically new mode of existence. Instead of wandering across a large territory and feeding themselves by killing game and collecting berries, seeds and other foods, people began to live in small, year-round villages. While they still did some hunting and foraging, their sustenance increasingly came from domesticated animals and plants. The first farmers learned how to raise crops of wheat, barley, peas and beans, and they bred manageable cattle, sheep, goats and pigs from wilder stock. Villages grew larger and the farming more skillful, providing surplus food that would eventually give rise to what we call civilization—complex societies with specialized labor, writing, laws, art and much more. But well before that threshold was reached late in the fourth millennium B.C.E., wine had entered the picture of human progress.

THE TAMING OF THE VINE

At some point in the dim dawn years of farming, attention had turned to a certain vine known to botanists as *Vitis vinifera*—*Vitis* being the genus name for grapevines (a classification that includes about a hundred species) and *vinifera* the species name of this particular vine (it means "wine-bearing"). The woody, climbing plant was common enough, growing in temperate climates from Spain to Central Asia. Humans had undoubtedly long appreciated its fruit, which, as it ripens, accumulates a volume of sugar greater than that of other grapevine species—although far less than the modern, domesticated versions of *vinifera*. Occasionally, by happy accident, the vine may even have yielded a bit of wine back in hunter-gatherer days, the result of some ripe grapes being left in a container and rupturing, which allowed natural yeasts on the grapes' skins to go to work on the juice.

This Eurasian vine had deficiencies, however. Its fruit was small and full of seeds, and the skin of the grapes was tough. The reproductive habits of the wild vine also posed problems. Most of the plants were either male or female, and only the female version produced a significant amount of fruit—and only if it was fertilized by the pollen of a male. Early attempts to cultivate the vine presumably involved planting the seeds of the fruitful female plants and destroying the nonproductive males—a blind alley, since the females would then become barren as well. Fortunately, a small fraction of the wild vines were hermaphrodites, with flowers of both sexes, and thus able to reliably fruit on their own. These plants, whose seedlings tended to carry on the hermaphroditic trait, offered a workable path to domestication. Because they were consistently productive, they would have been favored for cultivation. Improvements presumably followed as the early farmers noticed which of the hermaphrodites yielded abundant, high-quality fruit or had other desirable traits.

The biblical patriarch Noah, said to have planted the first vineyard after surviving the Flood, lies drunken beside a wine barrel. This marble relief of his moment of shame was created by the fourteenth-century Florentine artist Andrea Pisano.

A fundamental problem remained, however. As it happens, all grapevines tend to vary markedly from one generation to the next in their normal, sexual mode of reproduction, meaning that a favorable trait might quickly be lost. But, possibly very early in the domestication process, a way around this unpredictable behavior was discovered. By propagating a vine with rootings or cuttings, its genetic makeup could be preserved: The next generation would be clones of the mother vine. Using this method, faithful replication of a particular set of traits could thus be maintained for centuries. Moreover, since cuttings were readily transportable, cultivation of any particular clone could be expanded far beyond its point of origin without difficulty, as long as the growing conditions were suitable.

Over time, mutations and crossings of different genetic lines produced an extremely broad spectrum of clonal varieties: vines differing in leaf size, in soil or water preferences, and in temperature tolerance; grapes diverse in color, size, shape, acid or sugar content, aroma, taste, skin toughness and other characteristics. Progress was achieved mainly by trial and error, but *Vitis vinifera* proved wonderfully malleable. An estimated ten thousand different clonal types derived from the wild Eurasian vine are cultivated around the world today.

In seeking to pinpoint where the vine was tamed, scholars have examined several sorts of evidence. Grape seeds, or pips, are often found at archeological sites, and their shape can indicate whether they came from a wild or domesticated vine. Statistical analysis of DNA in vines today can help trace descent. And even the linguistic roots of such words as wine or grape offer some tantalizing clues. At present, leading candidates for first domestication include the Taurus Mountains of eastern and central Turkey, Transcaucasia (embracing modern-day Georgia, Armenia and Azerbaijan) and, just to the south, the foothills of the Zagros Mountains in Iran.

The story of Noah in the Old Testament jibes with this, at least approximately. After the biblical Flood, the ark "came to rest upon the mountains of Ararat," says the Book of Genesis. "Noah was the first tiller of the soil. He planted a vineyard, and he drank of the wine, and became drunk, and lay uncovered in his tent," later cursing one of his sons, Ham, for witnessing his nakedness. What intrigues investigators of the origins of viniculture is the mention of Ararat. That is the name of the highest mountain in the Caucasian ranges that stretch between Turkey and Iran to Armenia and Georgia.

As with domestication, learning how to systematically make wine from vinifera grapes would have been a slow learning process. Probably it had to await the appearance of pottery vessels, which occurred sometime in the late seventh millennium B.C.E. Such vessels were needed as a container for fermenting the juice and also for minimizing the exposure of wine to air.

A broken piece of pottery found in the Zagros Mountains of Iran and dated to about 5400 B.C.E. is one of the oldest archeological proofs of winemaking. The fragment, excavated from the earthen floor of a small mud-brick dwelling at a site called Hajji Firuz Tepe, belonged to a long-necked, undecorated jar with a capacity of about nine liters. On it was a yellowish

The story of Noah is echoed in several Near Eastern legends, including that of King Jamshid of Iran, credited with growing the first wine grapes after receiving seeds from a magical bird. The mythic king—here seen raised on his throne by demons on the first day of spring—is described in Persian literature as a font of wisdom: He instructed humankind in such fundamental skills as spinning and weaving, devised cures for illnesses and initiated seafaring.

deposit left by some vanished liquid. Recently, in a laboratory at the University of Pennsylvania Museum, this stain was subjected to sophisticated chemical analysis by Dr. Patrick McGovern, a leading authority on wine in the ancient world and a pioneer of the field known as molecular archeology. One of the compounds detected by the analysis was tartaric acid. Since grapes are the only significant source of that particular acid in the Near East, finding it in the deposit strongly suggested that the jar had once held wine. What virtually clinched the case was the presence of a second telltale compound, this one indicating that the liquid in the jar had been mixed with a tree resin. Resins are natural bactericidal agents, serving to protect trees from attack by microorganisms when their bark is torn. In the ancient world, they were commonly added to wine to fend off acetic acid bacteria, the microorganism responsible for turning wine into vinegar if it is exposed to air. (Retsina, the Greek wine flavored with pine resin, carries on that tradition.) For further protection against the souring bacteria, the narrow neck of the Hajji Firuz Tepe jar would have been sealed with a stopper. All in all, the pottery fragment provided clear testimony that winemaking was well underway by the sixth millennium B.C.E.

Above: Chemical analysis of a residue in the jar above—one of six found in a Neolithic house in the hamlet of Hajji Firuz Tepe in Iran—revealed that it held wine seven millennia ago.

Right: Archeologist Mary Voigt (white hat on the left) of the University of Pennsylvania Museum supervises the excavation of the room where the jars were set in the floor along one wall. Remnants of a fireplace and other vessels that were evidently used for storing and preparing foods indicate that this space served as a kitchen. The house also included two storage rooms and a large room that probably doubled as living and sleeping quarters for an extended family.

Opposite: Not far from the site of Hajji Firuz Tepe in the foothills of the Zagros Mountains of Iran, a river winds past hillside vineyards.

An Ancient Nexus of Wine

5400–5000 B.C.E. wine jar from Hajji Firuz Tepe, Iran

3300 B.C.E. bird-shaped vase from Uruk, Mesopotamia

3000 B.C.E. kneeling wine bull, Elam

2950 B.C.E. wine jar (amphora) with mud seal, Egypt

2600 B.C.E. wine cup from Ur, Mesopotamia

1750 B.C.E. electrum beaker with birds on the rim, Afghanistan

1100 B.C.E. gav, a wine bull from Marlik, Iran

685 B.C.E. wine jug from Urartria (Armenia)

645 B.C.E. Ashurbanipal's queen with wine cup under a grape vine arbor, Nineveh, Assyria

540 B.C.E. takuk, a silver drinking horn (rhyton) from Achaemenian Iran.

535 B.C.E. kylix, a Greek wine cup

C. 350 C.E. gazelle takuk (rhyton) from Sasanian Iran

C. 550 bolboleh, a decanter that sings like a songbird as it pours out wine, from Iran

C. 1250 khorus, a decanter in the form of a rooster, from Iran

C. 1430 agate wine cup, Herat, Afghanistan

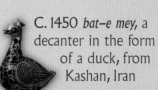

C. 1450 bat–e mey, a decanter in the form of a duck, from Kashan, Iran

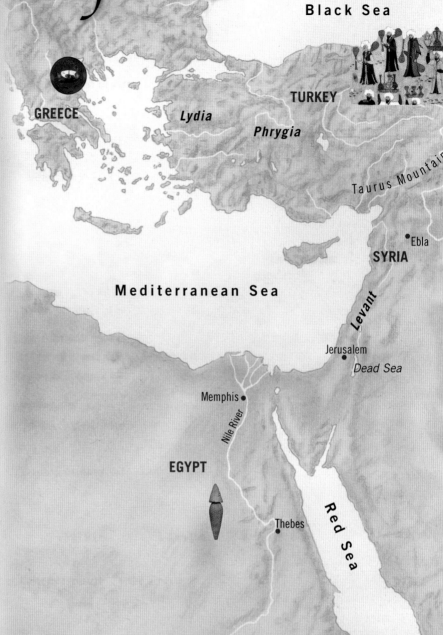

The immense Iranian plateau lies north and east of the Persian Gulf. It rises from the alluvial plains of Mesopotamia but is set apart from them by the Zagros mountain chain, source of the Karun, Dez and Karkheh Rivers that flow down into the confluence of the Tigris and Euphrates Rivers, called the Shatt al-Arab, which empties into the Persian Gulf. The plain of Susiana, west of these great mountains, was settled in the late sixth millennium B.C.E. by farming and livestock-raising peoples. This area was geographically an extension of the Tigris and Euphrates river valleys, and was culturally and politically connected to

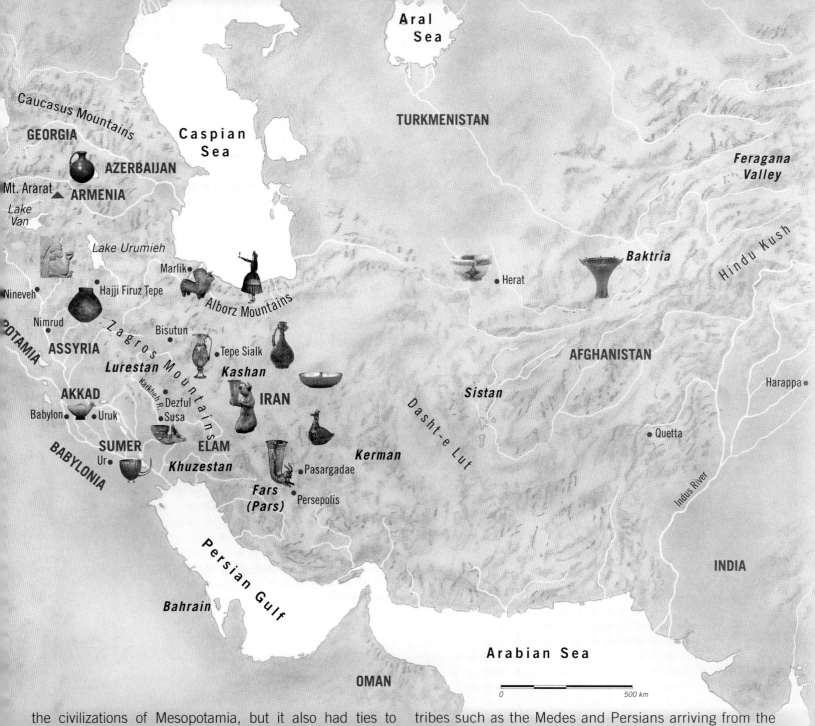

the civilizations of Mesopotamia, but it also had ties to peoples who descended from the northern mountain valleys of Lurestan and from the southeastern Iranian plateau in Fars. The highland region in the southeast became the cradle of Elamite civilization, whose chief city Susa was occupied more or less continually from about 4000 B.C.E. Archeological evidence, rituals and traditions bespeak a rich and close relationship between the people of this area and winemaking and drinking. Around 1500 B.C.E., the Iranian plateau became the homeland of Indo-European tribes such as the Medes and Persians arriving from the Eurasiatic steppes. In the Achaemenian empire of the fifth century B.C.E., Darius the Great considered himself to be of Iranian (Aryan) stock, and Iranian countries in his empire occupied a special position, but he called himself "a Persian from Persia" (Pars, now called Fars). By the third century C.E., however, royal identity had broadened: The Sasanian ruler Shapur I referred to himself as "king of the kings of the Iranians" *(shah-an shah-e Iran)*.

C. 1550
Turkish glass
blowers

C. 1550 *qadah–e dust gani*, a friendship wine bowl, from Safavid Iran

C. 1800 Qajar girl
with wine glass

OUTWARD BOUND

From its birthplace somewhere in the northern uplands of the Near East, the domesticated vine, along with winemaking skills, spread to Egypt by about 3000 B.C.E., to Crete and Greece a millennium later, and thence on through Europe. The Greeks said that viniculture was the gift of the god Dionysus (Bacchus to the Romans), whose cult engaged in ritualistic wine drinking. According to legend, this wine god had traveled extensively through lands to the east and south before reaching Greece—an intriguing echo of the historical truth. The Athenian playwright Euripides gave voice to Dionysus in the *Bacchae:*

> *I have come a long way. From Lydia and Phrygia,*
> *The lands of the golden rivers,*
> *Across the sun-baked steppes of Persia,*
> *Through the cities of Bactria [present-day Afghanistan],*
> *Smiling Arabia, and all the Anatolian coast,*
> *Where the salt seas beat on turreted strongholds*
> *Of Greek and Turk. I have set them all dancing;*
> *They have learned to worship me*
> *And know me for what I am:*
> > *A god.*
> *And now,*
> *I have come to Greece.*

But wine didn't gain a firm foothold everywhere. It was an also-ran among beverages in Lower Mesopotamia, where writing and other hallmarks of civilization first emerged at the end of the fourth millennium. There, by far the most popular drink was beer, brewed mainly from fermented barley. Because grapevines couldn't be grown on the hot, dry alluvial plains of the region, wine had to be imported, which made it too expensive for mass consumption. Still, considerable amounts reached the thriving lowland cities of Mesopotamia from producers in Transcaucasia and Iran, arriving both by overland routes and rivers.

In the fifth century B.C.E. the Greek historian Herodotus, who traveled widely in the Near East, explained how wine was shipped to Babylon in Lower Mesopotamia.

> The vessels…are round and made all of skins. For they make ribs of the willows that grow in Armenia, above Babylon. The vessels thus made like shields they fill with reeds and use for carrying merchandise down the river, generally palm-wood casks of wine.

Apparently these boats could handle about twenty-five tons of cargo. Prevented by strong currents from returning upstream, they were taken apart at their destination. The ribs and reeds were sold, and the skins, destined for new vessels, were returned to Armenia on the backs of donkeys that had been part of the cargo.

By the time Herodotus was writing about the area, a vigorous wine trade had been plied in Mesopotamia and Iran for more than two thousand years, even if it benefited only the elite. Small city-states exacted tolls as the wine traveled toward

According to a Homeric hymn illustrated on this
cup (sixth century B.C.E.), the wine god Dionysus
was seized by pirates during his journey to Greece.
He promptly broke his bonds, caused grape vines
to spring from the mast and transformed himself
into a lion. The terrified pirates jumped into the
sea, whereupon he turned them into dolphins.

THE TEARS OF HORUS

In the closing years of the fourth millennium B.C.E., not long after the peoples of the eastern edge of the Fertile Crescent led humankind into the historical era, another great civilization arose, this one in the land watered by the Nile. The elite of Egypt were enamored of wine from the start. Domesticated vines, imported from Canaan, grew well in the rich soil of the Nile Delta, and the Egyptians developed sophisticated winemaking skills—shown in detail in some tomb paintings done for pharaohs and high officials. Such paintings, along with tangible funerary articles, were a kind of magical way of transferring the comforts of this world to the afterlife.

The Egyptians were inventive in all phases of viniculture. For easy harvest, vines were trained over pergolas or propped up by poles to form a natural canopy. The slippery job of trampling the harvested grapes to extract their juice was performed by workers who supported themselves by hanging onto ropes or overhead bars. Additional juice was pressed from the skins by putting them in an elongated linen sack and twisting the two ends in opposite directions with poles. All the juice was promptly put in jars, where most of the fermentation took place. The jars were stoppered with a pottery lid and partially sealed with a mound of clay. Small, temporary holes left in the clay allowed the fermentation

gases to escape; these holes were then closed and the clay stamped with the mark of the estate.

Wine was associated with several gods, especially Osiris, who might be addressed as "lord of wine at flooding." Sometimes wine was called the "sweat of Re" (the sun god) or "the tears of Horus"—Horus being a falcon-headed god, representative of the pharaoh, whose eyes were described as grapes from which wine flowed. Ritual libations with wine were important in the life of ancient Egypt, but wine drinking for pleasure was hardly neglected: Some tomb paintings show banquets where the guests are imbibing freely—yet another delight of this world that was hoped for in the next.

A wall painting in a tomb dating to about 1400 B.C.E. details some of the stages of winemaking: harvesting grape clusters from vines trained over poles or a pergola (not shown); the crushing of grapes underfoot by workers who maintain their balance with hanging straps; and the collection of juice for fermentation and storage in large pottery vessels. At right is an early Egyptian wine jar, dating to about 2950 B.C.E. Made from coiled strips of clay and incised on the shoulders with hieroglyphs indicating the contents, it was closed with a pottery cap, then tightly sealed with a conical mass of clay.

This silver wine beaker, vividly decorated with horses and winged lions attacking rams, came from a grave at Marlik, a center of the Amlash culture of northwest Iran in the late second and early first millennia B.C.E. Some Assyrian influence is seen in the work of Amlash artisans, but they developed their own distinctive styles.

its markets, and in some places, merchants organized themselves into guilds to control the flow. Consumption could be prodigious at the royal level: In one palace, a series of long rooms held rows of lidded wine jars, each about three feet in height—truly a cellar worthy of a king.

The wine shipments had considerable variety: Cuneiform sources mention red wine, white (or clear) wine and sweet wine, and they also describe wines as "strong" or "early." But these categories merely touch the surface of wine's variability in the ancient world. Along with tree resins, many different spices and herbs were frequently added to wine—rosewater, saffron, capers, and pepper, among them. Wine might be mixed with honey or barley malt. It was often diluted with water. It could be boiled down to increase its sweetness. Such treatments could serve a number of purposes: preserving the wine, enhancing its perceived medicinal value, giving it some desired taste, or disguising poor quality. But additives and other manipulations, while common, were by no means universal. Sometimes wine was left alone and enjoyed, perhaps after improvement by aging, as a pure expression of the grape.

In the ancient Near East, anyone seeking to please a king would present him with a gift of fine wine—a measure of the esteem in which it was held. By the same token, wine figured in displays of royal magnanimity. Around 870 B.C.E., for example, Ashurnasipal II, ruler of Assyria, served vast quantities of wine in a ten-day banquet put on to inaugurate his new capital of Nimrud. It was quite an affair. According to the official records, 69,574 people attended. They consumed 1,000 fattened cattle, 1,000 calves, 10,000 sheep, 15,000 lambs, 500 gazelles, 20,000 doves, 10,000 fish, and a great deal more besides. To slake the thirst of the attendees, 10,000 jars of beer were served and—much more impressive—10,000 skins of wine, which was about ten times as expensive as the beer. Reliefs show guests sitting on couches and drinking the wine from shallow bowls as attendants stand by with jugs ready for refills.

In palaces of the Urartian culture of present-day Armenia and Azerbaijan, jugs like this one (seventh century B.C.E.) were used to transfer small amounts of wine from huge storage jars that each held over a thousand gallons. The Urartians—neighbors and potent rivals of the Assyrians—vanished from history in the sixth century B.C.E., probably overrun by the Medes of northern Iran.

With musicians and servants attending them in this frieze (seventh century B.C.E.), Assyria's King Ashurbanipal and his queen sip wine in an arbor at Nineveh. The wine cellars of Assyrian rulers were immense and provided a liquid form of pay to the palace staff as well as serving royal pleasure.

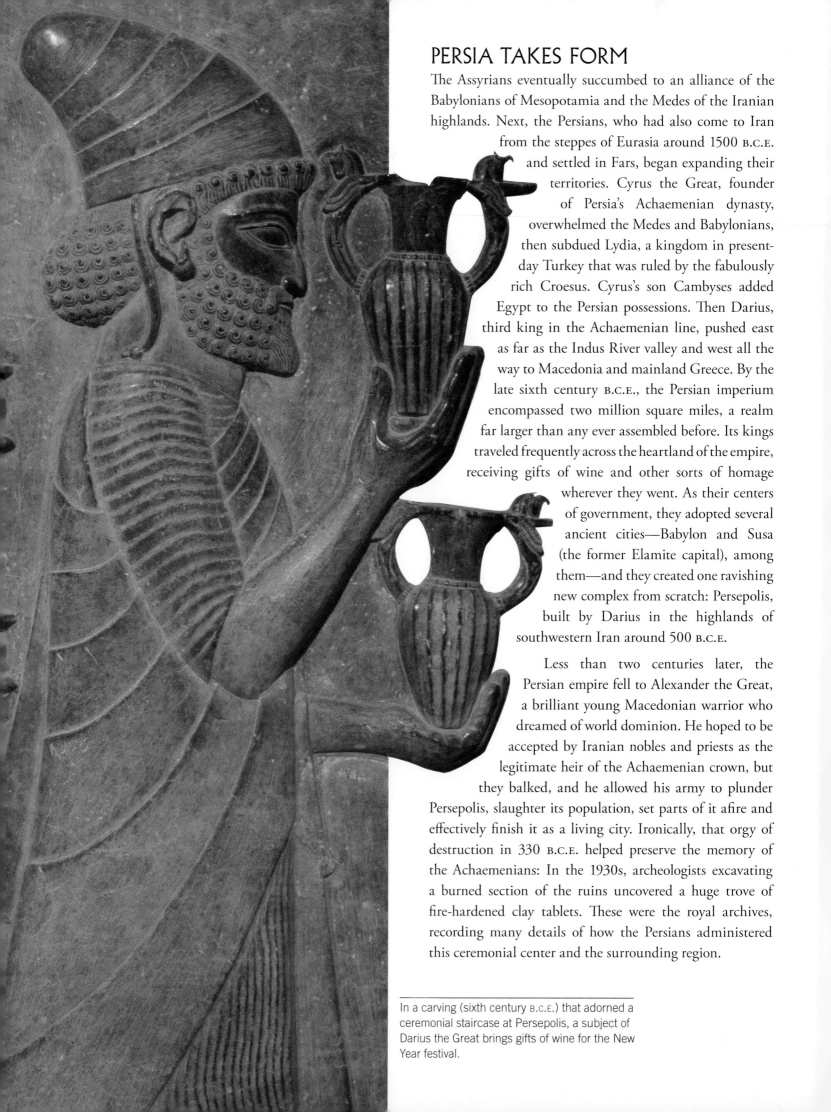

PERSIA TAKES FORM

The Assyrians eventually succumbed to an alliance of the Babylonians of Mesopotamia and the Medes of the Iranian highlands. Next, the Persians, who had also come to Iran from the steppes of Eurasia around 1500 B.C.E. and settled in Fars, began expanding their territories. Cyrus the Great, founder of Persia's Achaemenian dynasty, overwhelmed the Medes and Babylonians, then subdued Lydia, a kingdom in present-day Turkey that was ruled by the fabulously rich Croesus. Cyrus's son Cambyses added Egypt to the Persian possessions. Then Darius, third king in the Achaemenian line, pushed east as far as the Indus River valley and west all the way to Macedonia and mainland Greece. By the late sixth century B.C.E., the Persian imperium encompassed two million square miles, a realm far larger than any ever assembled before. Its kings traveled frequently across the heartland of the empire, receiving gifts of wine and other sorts of homage wherever they went. As their centers of government, they adopted several ancient cities—Babylon and Susa (the former Elamite capital), among them—and they created one ravishing new complex from scratch: Persepolis, built by Darius in the highlands of southwestern Iran around 500 B.C.E.

Less than two centuries later, the Persian empire fell to Alexander the Great, a brilliant young Macedonian warrior who dreamed of world dominion. He hoped to be accepted by Iranian nobles and priests as the legitimate heir of the Achaemenian crown, but they balked, and he allowed his army to plunder Persepolis, slaughter its population, set parts of it afire and effectively finish it as a living city. Ironically, that orgy of destruction in 330 B.C.E. helped preserve the memory of the Achaemenians: In the 1930s, archeologists excavating a burned section of the ruins uncovered a huge trove of fire-hardened clay tablets. These were the royal archives, recording many details of how the Persians administered this ceremonial center and the surrounding region.

In a carving (sixth century B.C.E.) that adorned a ceremonial staircase at Persepolis, a subject of Darius the Great brings gifts of wine for the New Year festival.

WINE TO WELCOME THE NEW YEAR

Inscriptions on some of the tablets found in the ruins of Persepolis indicate that wine libations figured in ceremonies held at the spring equinox to celebrate the New Year. In Persian households, it became customary to include a bowl of wine among the articles assembled for Nowruz, as the New Year festival is called. After the coming of Islam, this was gradually replaced with vinegar. To this day, however, in some Iranian families the head of the family offers a sip of wine to everyone present, including the children, at the moment of transition, when the old year gives way to the new.

HAFEZ

Some tablets dealt with the distribution of wine. By royal authority, it went to a substantial proportion of the population, with amounts carefully calibrated according to rank. Members of the king's own family were issued about five quarts per day, although much more would be forthcoming on the occasion of a banquet; one entry in the archives tells of a princess getting a shipment of five hundred gallons. Officials, members of the royal guard and various functionaries took some of their salary in wine. Ordinary workers received a monthly allowance of ten to twenty quarts. And women of the working class were rewarded with wine if they added to the labor force: When a male child was born, the mother received ten quarts; a girl baby warranted only half as much.

For the inhabitants of Persepolis, the wine rations and rewards came mostly from highland vineyards a short journey to the northeast. That locale, where the city of Shiraz later rose, was renowned for its wines, a reputation that would only grow with time. In the fourteenth century C.E., Shiraz would be the home of the great poet Hafez, whose verses celebrate the drinking of wine.

Hafez and other poets often alluded to a legend crediting the discovery of winemaking to a Persian king named Jamshid. In a particularly vivid version of the tale, King Jamshid one day saw a bird (symbol of good) being strangled by a snake (symbol of evil). After the king had the snake killed, the bird brought him some bright green seeds in return for his kindness. Jamshid ordered them planted in the royal gardens, and there they grew into vines that produced many blue berries. When the king drank some of the juice of the berries, he found it bitter and declared that it was poison. Later, a beautiful slave girl—one of his favorites—decided to kill herself with the liquid because she was suffering terrible headaches. She drank several glasses, fell asleep and awoke cured. She told the king what had happened, and he decided to try the drink again. This

An elliptical silver-and-gilt wine bowl (sixth or seventh century C.E.) is decorated with images of the magical bird that brought grape seeds to the legendary king Jamshid for the first vineyard.

time, he enjoyed it so much that he recommended it to his people as a medicine—a usage that, in actuality, it has always had in Persian culture: Some Persian synonyms for wine are *shah daru* (king's medicine), *nush daru* (wine medicine), *daru-ye gham* (medicine for grief) and *bihush daru* (medicine that makes you unconscious).

Hafez paid homage to King Jamshid in a poem addressed to a "saqi" (wine server):

> *Saqi! Come, that wine that rapture bringeth,*
> *Give me. For I, much heart-bereft, have fallen;*
> *Saqi come. That wine, wherefrom the cup of Jamshid,*
> *Boasteth of seeing into nonexistence.*
> *Give me, so that by the aid of the cup,*
> *I may be like Jamshid,*
> *Ever acquainted with the world's mystery.*

In truth, various Iranian peoples had been making wine on a large scale long before the Persians arrived. Seeds of domesticated vines dating to the late fourth millennium B.C.E. have been found several hundred miles northwest of Persepolis, at the site where the Elamites established their mountain capital, and much evidence traces the spread of viniculture to other parts of Iran over the next two millennia. But in Persian culture, wine had a particularly central role.

According to Iranian scholar Homa Nateq, the wine server's basic title, *saqi,* is derived from the Persian word *shakhi,* which literally means "horn carrier." It harks back to a very remote time when the people of the inner Asian steppes and around the Caspian Sea were mainly stockbreeders. Periodically they sacrificed a bull and drank its blood to win the favor of the gods. The memory of such sacrificial rites found expression in Zoroastrianism, a quasi-monotheistic religion that may have emerged as early as 1000 B.C.E. Zoroastrians held that the supreme god, Ahura Mazda, created a bull and then sacrificed it to produce all other animals. At the end of time, the sacrifice of another bull would bring immortality to the blessed.

بیا ساقی آن می که حال آورد   کرامت فـــــزاید کمال آورد

به من ده که بس بیدل افتاده‌ام   وزین هر دو بی‌حاصل افتاده‌ام

بیا ساقی آن می کز او جام جم   زند لاف بینائی اندر عدم

به من ده که گردم به تأیید جام   چو جم آگه از سرّ عالم تمام

A ram's head terminates an Achaemenian terra-cotta wine horn dating to about 500 B.C.E. The concept of a horn as a wine vessel was adopted by the Greeks. Of the discovery of wine, the Greek playwright Nonnos wrote in *Dionysiaca*, "The fruit bubbled out red juice with white foam. They scooped it up with oxhorns, instead of cups which had not yet been seen, so that ever after the cup of mixed wine took this divine name of winehorn."

Terra-cotta wine vessels used by the Amlash culture of northwestern Iran in the late second millennium B.C.E. included the wine bull or *gav* (below) and the wine leg or *pa-ye sharab* (far right). The wine leg had holes in the feet that were unplugged to dispense the contents. The silver-and-gold Sasanian cup opposite was crescent-shaped in profile and symbolized the moon. Filling it with wine represented the conjunction of the sun and moon.

Wine became a symbolic substitute for the blood of the bull, possibly when Zoroastrianism was adopted as the religion of the Persian court. In ritual libations, the wine was poured into cups from vessels shaped like animals, betokening the ancient practice of sacrifice. Some of the vessels had a horn-like form, with the head of an animal at the pointed end. Others represented the full figure of a bull, a duck or a rooster. Called *takuk* in Persian and rhytons in English (from the Greek), animal-shaped vessels would remain in use in Iran for many centuries, almost to the verge of modern times. Wine was also dispensed from containers called "wine legs," whose ritual significance is unknown. In addition, drinking sets for banquets and ceremonies included beautifully crafted bowls, jars, ladles and other paraphernalia.

Wine's religious meaning was not limited to symbolizing blood. Zoroastrianism associated the god Ahura Mazda with light and the sun, and wine was construed as a kind of liquid embodiment of solar radiance. Analysis of literary and archeological evidence by A. S. Melikian-Chirvani of the Center for Scientific Research in Paris yields a picture of rituals performed by magian masters—members of the hereditary class of Zoroastrian priests—in which the symbology of light and blood are both invoked. Just before dawn and also at sunset, the magi would pour wine libations from bull-shaped vessels into crescent cups resembling boats. As daylight waxed or waned, the wine was drunk, just as the blood of a bull had been.

Most wine was, of course, consumed for pleasure. Cyrus, first of the Achaemenians, was exceedingly fond of it according to Xenophon, another Greek chronicler who traveled in the Near East. "The Persian king has vintners scouring every land to find some drink that will tickle his palate; an army of cooks contrives dishes for his delight." When the king drank a good wine, he would dispatch his half-empty jar to a friend, along with the message: "For some time Cyrus had not found a pleasanter wine than this one; and he therefore sends some to you, begging you to drink it today with those whom you love best."

Among the Persians, wine was even seen as an aid to good decision making. According to Herodotus, "It is their general practice to deliberate on weighty matters when they are drunk; and in the morning when they are sober, the decision which they came to the night before is put before them by the master of the house in which it was made; and if it is then approved of, they act on it; if not, they set it aside." The wine server played a key role: He abstained from wine during the night of drinking and acted as a kind of recording secretary for the proceedings.

According to several Greek and Roman observers, a Persian king ate his meals alone behind a curtain, but afterward, others joined him to sip wine, talk and listen to music.

Although the king was unique in this solitary mode of dining, the custom of separating meals and wine drinking was a fixture of Persia culture. After a meal was finished, Persians would brush their teeth, eat springs of basil to freshen their breath, and set up a new table, usually in the garden, where wine was accompanied by small savory and sweet dishes: grape leaves with various stuffings; dumplings stuffed with meat; *kuku*s (egg frittatas); spicy, aromatic meatballs; *borani*s (mixtures of yogurt and vegetables); bread and cheese with fresh herbs and nuts; fruit; pomegranate arils with angelica petals and salt; hemp seeds roasted with gazelle fat; and dates stuffed with pistachios or walnuts. This second table was the place for conversation and socializing, a time to relax and savor the company of friends and family.

A DISSENTING VIEW

Some of the medieval Persian poets who extolled wine drinking did not like the age-old custom of separating it from the main meal—particularly the eating of kebabs without wine. One who felt this was Manuchehri, who wrote:

When those who know what's what
    Get together to dine,
We want three things, no more:
    Kebabs, and music, and wine;
But snacks? Or books of poems?
    Or backgammon? These we decline:
Backgammon's strictly for hovels,
    Books in schoolrooms are fine,
And snacks belong in bazaars.
    No, we find we confine
Our requirements to three:
    Kebabs, and music, and wine.

Manuchehri/Davis

THE WINE SERVER'S ROLE

From earliest times, wine was served at formal Iranian ceremonies by a toast-master. This role was performed by the magian master (a Zoroastrian priest), whose role, though not documented in the Zoroastrian scriptures, is depicted in scenes etched on ancient vessels (and kept alive by Persian poets after the coming of Islam). The magi believed that wine brought cheerfulness and that cheerfulness waged war against evil.

Later, this role was performed in Persian courts and aristocratic households by an individual called a *saqi* (from the Persian *shakhi*—horn carrier. The position was so demanding that candidates had to train for the job from childhood. As described by tenth- and eleventh-century poets whose verses often revolved around the gift of the grape, a *saqi* was expected to possess many talents and virtues beyond professional competence in cellar keeping and wine dispensing. His responsibilities included caring for musical instruments, since the music of the harp, lute, flute, tambour and female voice was a feature of wine drinking occasions. Most important of all, he was supposed to be a superb companion. The ideal wine server was young, good looking (usually a black-eyed beauty from Turkestan, with long hair tied back), amiable, possessed of perfect manners, knowledgeable about poetry (some would even write poetry), skilled in horsemanship and adept with weapons. According to the eleventh-century Persian statesman Nezam al-Molk, a candidate learned about wine drinking and became a *saqi* in the sixth year of his training. Synonyms used in poems suggest a sexual dimension to the role: Poets refer to the wine servers in such terms of endearment as *yar* (companion or sweetheart), *mah* (moon or a beauty), *bot* and *sanam* (idol) *kudak* (youth), and *Ahubazm* (gazelle party maker). Some wine servers rose to higher office, even becoming generals or governors.

The Persian poets described the proce-dure at important gatherings. The royal hall would be decorated with magnificent carpets and masses of flowers, and numerous musi-cians would be on hand, all of them wearing myrtle crowns. Ministers, military officers and nobles would sit in separate rows, while the king sat on a special throne. The *saqi* would bring a large decanter of wine from

Called a *takuk* in Persian, this fluted silver horn, decorated with the head and forequarters of a griffin, served both for drinking and pouring wine. A pair of holes in the chest of the griffin could either be closed by the fingers of a drinker or left open to allow wine to flow through. The wine horn shown here was made in Achaemenian Persia in around 500 B.C.E., but similar vessels remained in use in Iran long afterward and were also copied by Greek potters.

the cellar, put it in the middle of the group and fill everyone's goblet. Once everyone had a goblet of wine, he would say, *"Nush"* (from the Pahlavi word *"anush"* meaning "eternal life"), to which everyone present would reply, *"Nush-a nush, bash bash"* (Drink of eternal life, may it be so, may it be so). The *saqi* would then pass the wine around twice more. Each round had a particular meaning: The first represented good thoughts; the second, good words; and the third, good deeds. According to the Persian poets, however, the first round makes you happy and wakes you up; the second makes you brave and sensitive to the arts; the third brings out the best in you; the fourth and fifth will bring out your inner self, whether good or bad.

CEREMONIAL WINE DRINKING AND THE FRIENDSHIP BOWL

In ancient Iran, when the king drank with his knights *(jor'e khari)*, he would take the first sip from a common bowl called a friendship bowl *(qadah-e dust gani)*, which was then passed around by the *saqi* for all to vow fidelity and friendship *(namak giri)*. Versions of this vow-taking continued until quite recently. In more intimate gatherings *(majles-e ons)* someone would be chosen to perform the *saqi*'s role. He would usually be the wisest and most knowledgeable among the group because he was expected to know each person's capacity for wine and his talents. Traditionally, a jigger of wine would be thrown to the earth *(jor'e rizi)* at the start of the party to give back to the earth some of what had come from it and to cheer the souls of the dead. The connection between wine and death also figured in other ceremonies. Some wine would be sprinkled on the grave during a burial rite. In ancient times, the magi who were responsible for maintaining royal graves placed a little wine on the graves each day to make the dead man's soul happy. To this day in Iran the names of departed family and friends are engraved on the inside rim of Zoroastrian wine cups and the living toast the dead as they drink.

A sixteenth-century wine bowl bears an inscription from a poem by Hafez:

Here we are with our wine and the ascetics with their piety, let us see which one the beloved will take.

THE OLD ORDER CHANGES

The Achaemenian dynasty met its end at the hands of Alexander, but his rule did not last long. He died in 323 B.C.E. at the age of thirty-two, his end hastened by what was apparently an advanced case of alcoholism. The empire was then parceled out among several of his generals. For about two centuries Persia remained in the hands of a line of Hellenistic overlords called the Seleucids. They, in turn, were overthrown by the Parthians, a people who originated in eastern Iran. The Parthian rule eventually stretched from the borders of the emergent Roman empire—a perennial foe—to the lands of Central Asia.

Winemaking was very advanced in the eastern provinces of the Parthian realm—Fergana, Sogdia, and Bactria. The historian Strabo visited the Fergana Valley (in present-day Uzbekistan) and reported that the grapevines there were not only exceptionally productive but also yielded wine that did not have to be resinated to combat vinegar-causing bacteria. This marvelous wine, said Strabo, could profitably be aged for more than fifty years.

In 128 B.C.E., a Chinese general named Zhang Qian passed through the area on a diplomatic mission and was similarly impressed, noting, "They have wine made from grapes, and the wealthy store wine in large quantities up to ten thousand gallons, which keeps for several decades. The Persians are as fond of wine as their horses relish alfalfa." He carried domesticated *Vitis vinifera* seeds—as well as those of alfalfa—back to China, where both were unknown. The Chinese emperor received the imports enthusiastically, and extensive vineyards were soon planted near the imperial palace. Language preserves the link: In Chinese (and, later, Japanese), the word for grape wine is *budaw;* it derives from wine's Iranian name, *badeh.*

Meanwhile, Persian kings remained as devoted to the pleasures of wine as Cyrus had been. It was the lubricant of royal socializing.

This simple, subtly faceted glass bowl was produced by Sasanian craftsmen. Some of their glass wine bowls were carried to the Far East by merchants traveling along the Silk Road, and one has been found in the tomb of the sixth-century Japanese emperor Ankan.

In the third century C.E., the Parthians gave way to a new dynasty, the Sasanians, whose founders came from southwestern Iran, the same region that had produced the Achaemenians. While their choice of a location for an imperial capital was in Mesopotamia—at Ctesiphon, near present-day Baghdad—they built splendid palaces in the Persian heartland where Persepolis once stood, and they took every opportunity to remind their subjects of Persian glory of old. The imperial court glittered with proofs of wealth and exalted lineage. Food was presented on silver plates elaborately decorated with chase work or carvings. Wine was poured from animal-shaped vessels of gold and silver.

A fourth-century text titled *King Khosrow and His Knight* stressed that anyone hoping to find a position at the

A silver-and-gilt ewer from sixth-century Iran retains the bird shape of many far more ancient wine vessels but is decorated with females attaining religious ecstasy through wine. Because the flow of wine through the narrow neck produced a sound reminiscent of a songbird's call, this particular type of ewer was called a *bolboleh*, from the Persian word for the songbird, *bolbol*.

Sasanian court had to possess a thorough knowledge of the pleasures of the table, along with a familiarity with literature, history, music, chess and the military arts. In this coming-of-age manual, the king interrogates a young aspirant, asking him at one point, "Which wine is the best and finest?"

The lad replies by naming wines of several provinces: "May you be immortal! All these wines are good and fine: Kanik wine [uncooked wine], when it has been strained well, and the wine of Herat, and the wine of Marvruzi, and the wine of Bust, and the must [crushed grapes] of Alvand. But with the Assyrian wine and that of Fars province, no wine can stand the contest."

The king declared that this was the correct answer and hired the young man.

Opposite: Reclining by a stream with wine and musicians on hand, Shirin, an Armenian princess married to the Sasanian king Khosrow, admires a picture of her lover, Farhad. This three-way love story, written by the poet Nezami, was based on an ancient legend.

Below: A high-footed silver Sasanian bowl.

My friend, hold back your heart from enemies,
Drink shining wine with handsome friends like these;
With art's initiates let down your hair –
Stay buttoned up with ignoramuses.

Hafez/Davis

ای دوست دل از جفای دشمن درکش
با روی نکو شراب روشن درکش
با اهل هنر گوی گریبان بگشای
وز نااهلان قبای تمام دامن درکش

The Garden of Heavenly Creatures
(mid-sixteenth century).

THE RISE OF ISLAM

Sasanian rule reached all the way to the Arabian Peninsula by the sixth century C.E. There, Mohammad—future founder of a new faith—was born in the city of Mecca in 570 C.E. His impact would be immeasurable.

Not until the age of forty did Mohammad take up his calling as a prophet of God. His was the God of Moses and Abraham and Jesus, but without the overlay of Jewish dogma or Christian belief in the Resurrection. In a long series of visions, God spoke to the prophet Mohammad through the angel Gabriel, imparting the truths of Islam. The prophet shared the revelations with his disciples, who memorized them and later wrote them down. The Qur'an—the holy book of Islam—reached its authorized form fifteen years after Mohammad's death in 632 C.E. Its teachings would touch on almost every aspect of life, including the acceptability of alcohol.

In the early years of his preaching, Mohammad did not object to wine drinking, long a familiar part of daily life in Arabia. As time passed, his position changed—an evolution that can be traced in the Qur'an, which takes up the topic several times and in several different tones, increasingly focusing on the danger of drunkenness. (No such evil could occur in paradise, described as a lovely garden watered by fountains and streams, where the righteous would find "dark-eyed houris, chaste as hidden pearls" and "shall drink of a pure wine, securely sealed, whose very dregs are musk.") The four relevant verses of the Qur'an (opposite) first speak of wine as part of nature's plentitude, then link wine to gambling and sinfulness, then warn against praying when drunk and finally—in the verse that became the basis for prohibition—condemn wine as one of the "abominations devised by Satan." According to Islamic tradition, the last verse was God's reply when Mohammad sought guidance after some of his disciples quarreled violently during a drinking party.

By the time of Mohammad's death, Islam was the leading faith in most of Arabia. Soon afterward, nomadic tribesmen poured forth from the peninsula to spread the revealed truth by conquest. The Arabs swept across North Africa, through Palestine and Syria and Mesopotamia, north to Armenia. They razed the treasure-stuffed Sasanian palace at Ctesiphon in 642 C.E. and overran the cities of the Persian homeland. Eventually, Islam held sway from Portugal to the Indus River, all of it ruled from Damascus and later Baghdad by caliphs, Mohammad's successors as leaders of the faith. Throughout this dominion, alcohol was forbidden to believers. Wine production went on in many places, but it was relegated to Jews and Christians and was heavily taxed.

WHAT THE QUR'AN SAYS ABOUT WINE

The verses in the Qur'an that address the issue of wine drinking range from acceptance, to cautions about the dangers of drink, to a call for avoidance (although in language less absolute than, for example, the holy book's ban on eating pork).

We give you the fruit of the palm and the vine from which you derive intoxicants and wholesome food.
—Sura 16:69

They will ask you concerning wine and gambling. Answer, in both there is great sin and also some things of use unto men, but their sinfulness is greater than their use.
—Sura 2:219

Believers, do not approach your prayers when you are drunk, but wait till you can grasp the meaning of your words; nor when you are polluted—unless you are traveling the road—until you have washed yourself."
—Sura 4:46

Believers, wine and games of chance, idols and divining arrows are abominations devised by Satan. Avoid them so that you may prosper. Satan seeks to stir up enmity and hatred among you by means of wine and gambling and to keep you from the Remembrance of Allah and from your prayers. Will you not abstain from them?
—Sura 5:92

WHAT RUMI SAYS ABOUT WINE PROHIBITION

An interesting and very Iranian take on the Islamic banning of wine is provided in a poem by Jalal-al-Din Rumi in his *Masnavi*:

> *Evil won't always come*
> > *From a loss of self-control*
> *Wine makes a person ruder*
> > *Who has rudeness in his soul;*
> *A wise man when he drinks*
> > *Will seem to grow more clever,*
> *An evil-natured man*
> > *Will turn out worse than ever;*
> *But since most men's behavior's*
> > *An absolute disgrace*
> *Wine has become forbidden*
> > *To everyone, just in case!*

———————
Rumi/Davis

نه همه صالحی خوری شرم می کند   بر او دم بی سلامی جنان تری کند

دگر بو قلندر کو فر می شو   در بو بد خبری بستر می شو

لیک اغلب حسن بد پندونا   بر همه مرا محرم کم گراز

For the next six centuries, Persia remained under the nominal control of Arab caliphs. Their grip was sometimes challenged by local monarchs, and, in any event, their governance became increasingly Persian in style as the Arabs absorbed the older culture, developing an appreciation of its literature, architecture, cuisine and modes of entertainment. Wine drinking went on, especially among the elite, who found ways to justify it. One rationale emphasized wine's supposed medicinal properties. It was also argued that the Qur'anic ban applied only to overindulgence, which could interfere with proper worship. Another line of reasoning claimed that wine was permissible if diluted, making intoxication less likely. Or wine might be cooked—a procedure recommended in an Arabic couplet inscribed on some Iranian wine ewers:

It behooves you to drink cooked wine for it is
Licit provided it does not affect reason and understanding.

Marco Polo, the medieval traveler who ventured from Italy to China and back, took note of the cooking of wine but offered a different explanation: Wine was boiled, he said, to change its taste, which changed its name as well and allowed the wine to be drunk lawfully.

At times during the Arab caliphate, wine drinking was actually encouraged because of the tax revenues it produced. Even some of the leaders of the faith indulged: One caliph, fond of the color yellow, hung yellow satin on the walls of a room in his palace, added a decoration of oranges and melons, dyed fountain water yellow with saffron and held a party at which his guests were served only yellow wine.

This period saw the emergence of Persian poets who lauded wine drinking as a path to apprehending the divine and also as a rejection of the rigidity of the Islamic authorities. Often their verses had a melancholic or wistful quality. Hafez wrote in the fourteenth century:

At dawn, as tulips and narcissi opened,
I heard a plaintive ringdove sigh and weep there:
"Drink wine, since you'll be sober soon forever;
Up from the ground now! Soon enough you'll sleep there."

هنگام سحر که زنگ و لاشگفت
مرغ سحر به ناله و آه بگفت؛
می نوش که به نشاط جلوه هر بو
برخیز که در خاک بخسبی جلوه هر خفت

Wine ewers shaped to represent a rooster *(khorus)* may have appeared in Iran as early as 3000 B.C.E. Some were filled through the tail; the wine was poured from the beak and eyes. Zoroastrian tradition holds that the rooster is a companion of the angel Sorush, guardian of humankind at night. Because a rooster's crowing signaled the transition from evil darkness to the goodness of daylight, such ewers were used for a Persian wine drinking tradition known as *sabuh,* the morning cup of wine. The killing of roosters is still discouraged in some Zoroastrian communities.

A fascinating literary work written in the eleventh century by Amir Kaykavus, a Persian prince from Gorgan, was more practical about the issue. Intended as a guide for his son, it includes a whole chapter about wine drinking. "I neither urge you to drink nor can I tell you not to drink, since young men never refrain from action at anyone's bidding," he says. He then proceeds to offer much advice about when to drink (three hours after eating; never on Fridays or Saturdays, which are sacred; and only after the recitation of afternoon prayers on other days). He also has much to say about where to do it (preferably not in the open—and certainly never outside the home when intoxicated). And he sums up his position in a masterpiece of equivocation: "Wine drinking is a transgression;

if you wish to commit a transgression it should at least not be a flavorless one. If you drink wine, let it be the finest; if you listen to music, let it be the sweetest; and if you commit a forbidden act, let it be with a beautiful partner, so that even though you may be convicted of sin in the next world, you will at any rate not be branded a fool in this."

As a father, Kaykavus certainly was no fool.

PERSIAN ENDURANCE

Restraint in any form seemed alien to the next wave of conquerors, the Mongols. Led by the ruthless Genghis Khan, these horseback warriors swept in from the steppes of Asia in the year 1220. They leveled whole cities in the northeastern provinces of Persia and killed without mercy. A few decades later, the Mongols sacked the great city of Baghdad, slaughtered most of its population and deposed the Arab caliph.

The Mongols were epic drinkers. One of Genghis Khan's sons, his designated successor, died of alcoholism. In the lands that came under Mongol control, public drunkenness was commonplace, persisting even after the rulers converted to Islam. Hard drinking was also the custom of subsequent invaders from Central Asia—first the Ottomans, then the Timurids, led by Tamerlane, a warrior every bit as ferocious as Genghis Khan.

These were times of terrible suffering, made worse by epidemics and the destruction of irrigation systems. But soon after each invasion and the accompanying traumas, a subtle counterforce came into play. Like the Arabs before them, the people of the steppes found much in Persian culture to their liking. Those that stayed took up the ways of the world they had conquered.

Early in the sixteenth century, a new era began with the establishment of the Safavid dynasty, whose relationship with wine has been vividly documented by the historian Rudi Matthee. The Safavids hewed to an Iranian view of kingship that had its roots deep in the past. The ideal ruler was one who possessed both great martial ability and a vigorous appetite for wine, women and song. To be a fierce warrior and also to partake abundantly of life's pleasures were the qualities of a Persian king. The two sides of the coin were expressed in the phrase *razm o bazm*, which meant "fighting" and "feasting," respectively. The two activities might even be conjoined: Chronicles of kingly deeds from

Duck- or goose-shaped decanters *(bat-e mey)* date back to the first millennium B.C.E., and, as with rooster-shaped ewers, remained in use long afterward—a wine drinking tradition kept alive by Persian poets. This fifteenth-century example is filled through an opening behind the head; the wine is poured through the bill.

شیئی که با آب دیده همیشه مکرد وضو ∙ می بود همیشه منکر جام و سبو

در مجلس ما دوست بسی غو نا کرد ∙ او شیشه ما شکست و با تو بداو

Sasanian times onward tell of open-air feasts held both before and after a battle. In somewhat the same spirit, *bazm* was a frequent accompaniment of the favorite royal sport of hunting, a kind of sublimated *razm*.

Most ritual feasting was not associated with fighting at all. Much more often, the purpose was political—a standard exercise of kingship as the ruler traveled around his realm, always with an enormous entourage. A Portuguese diplomat described how Persians would visit the encampment of their monarch to pay homage:

> [He] would come out of his tent in his robe, with his sword on his belt, and immediately would drink a cup of wine to honor and welcome them. They would sacrifice a cow in front of him, clamoring that from now on no harm could come to them anymore. Those who had horses, mares or young girls would offer these to him. Following this they would leave for their districts, very satisfied and content.

Both in private and public, many Safavid kings drank wine in huge quantities. Persian chroniclers insisted that it had no effect; on the contrary, it demonstrated the king's physical strength and thus his fitness for rule. One king received this encomium: "Although he drinks incessantly from morning till evening, and from sunset to sunup, his face does not show the signs of drunkenness."

In a mid-seventeenth century drawing from Isfahan, the calligraphed couplets translate as:

That tearful sheikh, who piously forbade
The wine we drank while he devoutly prayed,
Brawled with the best of us last night – while he
Broke glasses, we broke all the vows he'd made.

Foreign visitors were struck by the fact that kings continued drinking even during Ramadan, the yearly period of fasting and prayer prescribed in the Qur'an. Nor was such behavior regarded as sinful by the kings' subjects, in part because the Safavids claimed descent from the son-in-law of the prophet Mohammad, Hazrat-e Ali. A French missionary in the seventh century wrote:

> The king calls himself the chief of religion, and the Persians hold that he cannot be damned or even judged, regardless of the sins he commits. They are not scandalized when he does not observe Ramadan and drinks wine, for they believe that he is without sin and exempt from all legal observations.

But royal drinking plainly got out of hand at times. In the throes of inebriation, one Safavid ruler grew so angry with a provincial governor that he had the man and two of his sons executed. Another king, in a drunken rage, reportedly ordered the blinding of his own brother. Several Safavid rulers drank themselves to death.

At times, the kings banned drinking by their Muslim subjects. The reasons were many: pressure from the Islamic clergy, a bid for divine favor as a war approached, a sense that public order was threatened by alcohol. The first Safavid to take this step, Tahmasb I, was a heavy drinker as a youth, then veered to the opposite extreme, personally forswearing alcohol and also ordering that taverns, liquor houses and brothels be closed throughout his realm. Punishments for disobedience were dire, and high rank was no protection, as exemplified by the powerful official who ignored the ban and was summarily stuffed in a barrel and thrown to his death from the top of a minaret.

I used to look for pleasure cautiously,
Now I drink wine and don't care who comes near –
I was afraid I'd lose my reputation,
Now that I've lost it what is there to fear?

Hasan Ghaznavi/Davis

یکچند نهان ز سُوی دلارام شدیم

و اکنون بعینیـان ز جهت می جام شدیم

رسیدن ماهمه ز بدنامی ماست

اکنون رِه پرسیم که بد نام شدیم

THE WARRIOR IDEAL

Over a period of thirty-five years in the late tenth and early eleventh centuries, the poet Ferdowsi composed what would come to be seen as the Persian national epic: the *Shahnameh* (Book of Kings), based on ancient legends and deeds. Heroic figures in Ferdowsi's narrative are men of prodigious appetite as well as great fighting prowess, a pairing of traits at the heart of the Persian concept of leadership. One story in the *Shahnameh* recounts a tragic conflict between Esfandyar, the son of a king, and Rostam, Iran's greatest hero. Prior to battle, they meet and talk. Finally Esfandyar says:

> *"There's no point in our boasting any more*
> *About our countless victories in war;*
> *Enough of who won what, and who was killed;*
> *The day's half done, we need our stomachs filled!*
> *Let them bring food for us, and while we eat*
> *No one's to talk of victory or defeat!"*
> *As Rostam ate the lamb they brought him there*
> *His appetite made all the others stare;*
> *Esfandyar said, "Serve him with uncooked wine,*
> *Let it affect him while we sit and dine,*
> *And when the wine has made his tongue grow loose*
> *We'll hear him chatter about King Kavus!"*
> *The steward brought a cup in which a boat –*
> *Or so it seemed – could have been set afloat...*

Rostam downs that portion and much more, saying that the wine has strengthened him in mind as well as body. He urges Esfandyar to be a friend, not a foe. But the prince, who will ultimately die at Rostam's hands, replies:

> *"Don't try to plant a seed that cannot grow!*
> *Tomorrow, when I've armed myself, you'll know*
> *Just what it is to face a noble knight:*
> *Don't praise yourself, go home, prepare to fight!*
> *Fighting or feasting I don't change; you'll see*
> *That wine and war are all the same to me..."*

Ferdowsi/Davis

Wine cup in hand, Rostam roasts a wild ass as Esfandyar's son Bahman looks on.

During the two centuries of the Safavid dynasty, many similar royal edicts were proclaimed. Although none were repealed, they all quietly lapsed. And, unlike Tahmasb I, most rulers never gave up wine entirely. One especially bibulous king—Solayman, the ruler said to have ordered the blinding of his brother—even took care to officially exempt his friends from a general ban. His reason for forbidding alcohol in the first place was a report that inebriated youths were making trouble near his palace; henceforth, said Solayman, anyone who indulged would have his belly cut open. But what went on at court was another matter. After all, a king needed friends to drink with. Royal permission to partake of wine was therefore granted to his drinking companions. (They imbibed in style. The wine bottles at Solayman's banquets were made of crystal and sometimes decorated with diamond studs.)

The most perceptive foreign observer of Safavid Persia was a French merchant and jeweler named Jean Chardin, who spent almost a decade traveling in the region in the second half of the seventeenth century. As might be expected of a Frenchman, his recollections of those years do not neglect the subject of wine. He reported that Persia's best wine came from grapes grown in vineyards around Shiraz, a highland city founded about a millennium earlier some thirty miles from the ruins of Persepolis. Virtually all of it was made by Jews and Armenians, who needed to be licensed by the king and the local governor. "It is not one of those strong wines which pleases the palate right away," Chardin wrote. "On the contrary, it appeared to me coarse the first time I drank it, but after I had drunk it a few days, it was preferable to all others and those who had become accustomed to it do not appreciate any other wine…Its color is the most attractive red and the most lively to be seen. It is, however, not a wine to keep long as it goes off after three years, because it is not fermented long enough and is bottled too early. On the other hand it does not deteriorate in transportation."

Much of the wine was shipped to distant markets, especially in India. The city of Shiraz was only a hundred miles from the coast and thus well positioned for this trade, which was mostly run by European shippers. Remarkably for that day, the wine made the trip in bottles, which were wrapped in straw and packed in cases to keep them secure en route.

Wine from the Shiraz region had been favored by Persian kings and their courts since the days of the Achaemenians, and the Safavids were no exception: About twelve hundred liters went to the royal cellars each year. Visitors from such prominent wine-producing countries as France or Spain regularly brought gifts of wine, but the rulers of Persia preferred what was made in their own dominion. (Georgia, part of the empire, was another excellent source.)

Although royal wine drinking grew increasingly private, it continued at court for as long as the Safavids ruled. Not surprisingly, the upper classes followed suit. As an Italian chronicler wrote early in the seventeenth century, "In Persia, though it is a country of Muslims, all drink wine with alacrity, without scruples or shame." By "all," he meant all of the elite, not the general population.

A young man picks grapes in a vineyard in Kholar, Shiraz.

SHAH ABBAS'S WINE CELLAR

In his account of his years in Iran during the seventeenth century, the French merchant and traveler Jean Chardin described where Shah Abbas, greatest of the Safavid kings, stored wine in his palace in Isfahan.

The building is like a kind of salon, some forty feet high, set two feet above ground level, built in the middle of a garden with a narrow entrance and screened by a small wall two feet away, making it impossible to see within. After entering, on the left-hand side are offices or stores, on the right a large room. It is surmounted by a vault which has the shape of a square or a Greek cross by means of two portals or arcades sixteen feet in depth which are along the sides. The center of the room is filled with a large water basin, the sides of which are made of porphyry. The walls are clad with slabs of jasper, eight feet high. Above, up to the middle of the vault are recesses made of a thousand different kinds of patterns, which are full of vases of all sorts of designs and materials imaginable.

In this ornamented salon, the floor is covered with rich gold and silk carpets. There is nothing more lively and entrancing than the countless variety of vases, cups and bottles of all kinds and shapes, designs and materials like crystal, cornelian, agate, onyx, jasper, amber, coral, porcelain, precious stones, gold, silver and enamel. All these are mixed with each other and seem as if they were encrusted along the walls. They appear so lightly attached as if they might fall from the vault. The storage along the sides of this superb room is filled with cases of wine. The wine is mostly in large bottles holding fifteen to sixteen pints or in bottles of two to three pints with a long neck.

One of the proverbs inscribed on the wall was:

> *"Life is a series of intoxicating states;*
> *Pleasure passes, hangovers remain."*

TOWARD MODERNITY

The dynasty ended in 1722 when an Afghan strongman captured Isfahan, the beautiful Safavid capital. More turbulence followed, and then another long-lived dynasty, the Qajars, took control in 1795. Winemaking went on, with any commercial production remaining almost exclusively in the hands of non-Muslims. Any exceptions were on a modest scale. A Viennese doctor named Jacob Eduard Polak, who served as Nasir al-din Shah's physician in the mid-nineteenth century, recounts that wine drinking parties were very discrete. Unlike the Safavids, the Qajars did not drink wine with foreigners but served them sherbets instead. Doctor Polak writes that the red wine of the Kholar region of Shiraz is of high quality, very alcoholic, and consumed locally as well as exported. For his part, the doctor often prescribed wine as a medicine, once recommending it to the foreign minister, a very conservative Muslim, as a cure for his malaria. The minister balked at first but finally agreed; according to Dr. Polak, his malaria was cured, and he became an avid disciple of wine's medicinal qualities. Dr. Polak also prescribed wine for the women in the shah's harem, whose lives were often miserable.

Wine production for strictly private purposes continued quietly all through the Qajar period. Recalling his boyhood in the early twentieth century, the eminent Iranian statesman Ghasem Ghani described his father's pursuit of winemaking as a hobby: "In the morning hours, father enjoyed visiting his vats of wine, which were kept in two cellars. Early in the morning he would see to all the vats himself. Later he would tell his friends that he had just opened such and such a vat, describing to them the wine's intoxicating rumbling and foaming; how this wine gleamed like a diamond or that batch shone ruby red."

The Qajar dynasty, grown corrupt and inept, ended in 1925. The following year, a former soldier crowned himself as Reza Shah and founded the Pahlavi dynasty. He set the country on a vigorous modernization path, which included upgrading winemaking practices. Among other steps, he brought in a German expert to set up an industrial-scale winery outside of Shiraz. The approach of the second world war and the British occupation of Iran put an end to this initiative, but in the decades after the war, wine production, sanctioned by the government, saw steady increases in both quantity and quality. New vineyards were planted, new wineries built and the latest technology adopted. One major winery—Pakdis—rose in western Iran near Lake Urumieh (Rezaieh), not far from the Neolithic village of Hajji Firuz Tepe, where some of the world's first winemakers plied their art more than seven millennia ago.

Since the Islamic Revolution of 1979, wine drinking has once again gone underground, yet it still has a cherished role in the social lives of many Iranians. Wine, indeed, is one of the oldest proofs of the resilience of Persian culture, flowing through history like an unstoppable river. More than a thousand years ago, Abu Nuwas, a poet in the caliph's court in Baghdad, spoke of wine as "the confidant of Time itself."

Intertwined lovers sip wine in a seventeenth-century painting from Isfahan.

It has been aged, such that if it were possessed of an eloquent tongue,
It would sit proudly amongst people and tell a tale of an ancient time...

Ancient indeed. Making its appearance in Iran at the very dawn of settled human existence, wine enlivened life in such early Iranian kingdoms as Elam; with the coming of Zoroastrianism, it took on religious meanings as a symbol of blood and light; it was deeply woven into the social and economic workings of Persepolis and later imperial capitals; through the centuries after the arrival of Islam, it held a place in Iranian courts and homes despite many bans; and, discreetly but deeply, it is part of Persianness today.

How fitting it is, then, that one of the world's great wine grapes honors this long and rich history with its name: Shiraz, also known as Syrah. The Shiraz grape is a mainstay of the huge Australian wine industry, finds expression in such celebrated French wines as Hermitage and is extensively cultivated in the United States, South Africa, Chile and Argentina. Since the ancestry of most grape varieties tends to be a tangled business, considerable uncertainty attends its origin. But for me, what matters is not where the grape comes from but the historical resonance of its name. It is a reminder of what wine has meant to Iran—and Iran to wine.

Wine is the opening key by which we find
Attributes hidden in the heart and mind:
The fox will be a lion when he drinks,
The timid man a hero; one who sinks
Beneath grief's weight finds joy, his cheeks will shine
Like pomegranates when he turns to wine.
The man who lifts his wine cup wants one thing —
The pleasure flutes and harps and singers bring.

Ferdowsi/Davis

به باده درون گوهر آید پدید

دل بسته را باده باشد کلید

چو بیدل خورد مو گردد دلیر

چو رو به خود گرد او شیر نر

چو غمگین خورد شاد مانه شود

به رخسار چون نار داله شود

هر آنکس که گیرد مداوار به جنگ

نخواهد هزار از رامش نای و چنگ

Jahangir, ruler of the Mughal empire in the early seventeenth century, commemorated his love of wine by minting a coin that showed him with cup in hand. Persian culture strongly influenced the Mughal court in India, reflecting the power of Jahangir's wife, a Persian princess, whom he called Nur-e Jahan (light of the world).

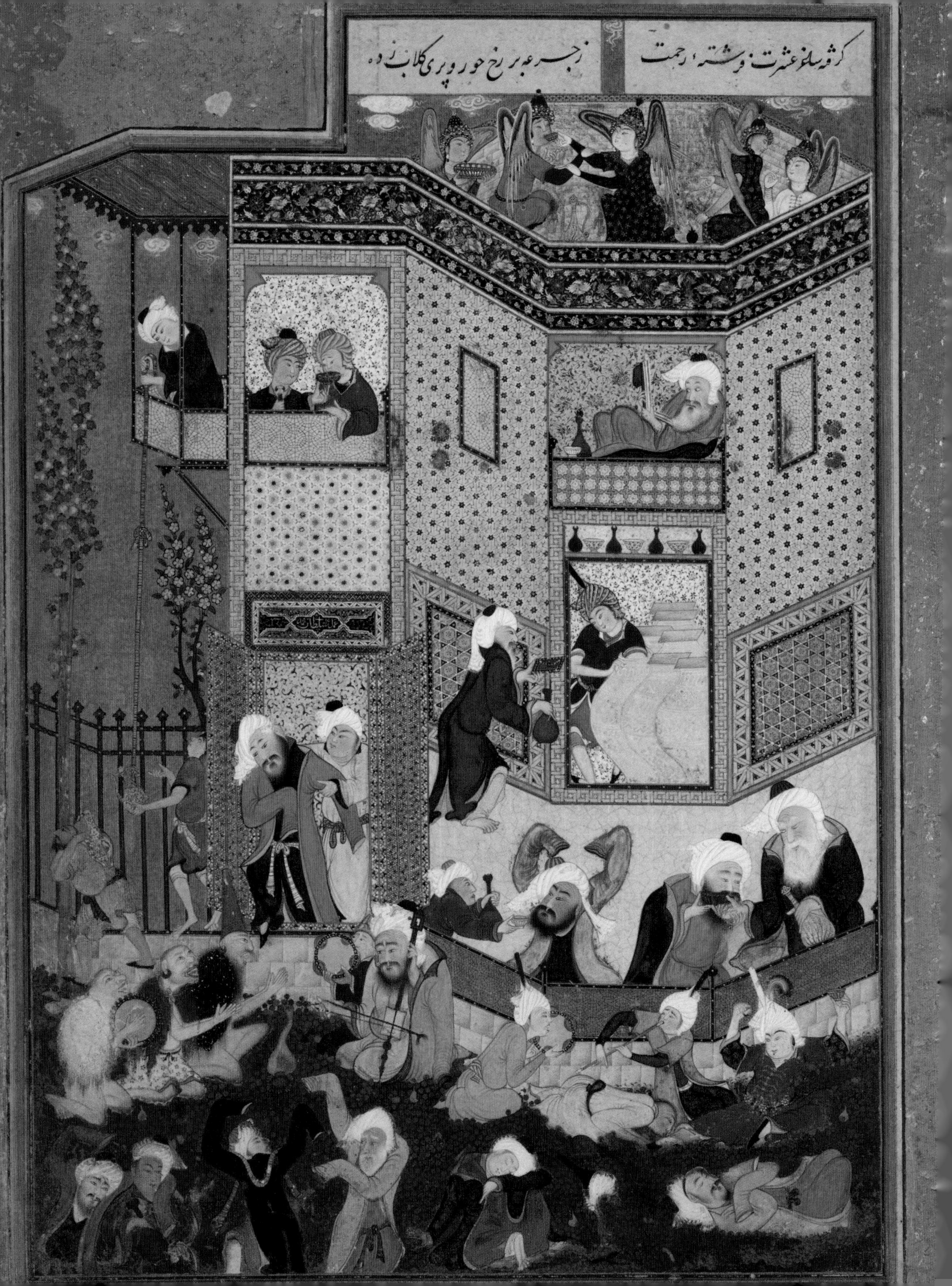
گرفته ساغر عشرت فرشتهٔ رحمت
ز جرعه بر رخ حور و پری گلاب زده

To drink good wine down and be happy – that's my way;
Ignoring faith and blasphemy – that's how I pray.
I asked the world to name her price, I'd marry her;
She said, "Your happy heart is what you'll have to pay."

———
Khayyam/Davis

مخوردن می شاد بوم کآئین منست
فارغ بودن زکفر ودین، دین منست
گفتم به عروس دهر کابینت چیست
گفتا دلِ خرم توکابین منست

WINE AND PERSIAN POETRY

Dick Davis

When we talk about Persian poetry we are referring almost exclusively to poetry written after the Arab invasion of the seventh century C.E., which brought the then new religion of Islam to the country. The reason for this is that very little poetry has come down to us from before the invasion, although we know that Iran had enjoyed a very vigorous pre-Islamic poetic culture, that included epic, romance and lyric verse.

The invasion led to a refashioning of the Persian language, which came to be written in a modified form of the Arabic script and which now incorporated many Arabic words, particularly in areas associated with learning and the arts of civilization. These last included the poetic culture: Virtually all the words in medieval and modern Persian to do with the technical aspects of poetry (meter, rhyme, metaphor and so forth) are Arabic in origin. And Persian poetry reemerged after the invasion under the shadow of Arabic poetry, adopting (and often adapting) its forms, technical devices and rhetorical strategies. Nevertheless it is clear from the earliest examples of Persian poetry, which are also (especially in the eleventh century) some of its greatest examples, that much of the old pre-Islamic culture still lingered in the culturally hybrid country that Iran had become.

Wine as a central subject of Persian medieval poetry is there from the beginning. By far the longest surviving poem of the first major Persian poet, Rudaki (a functionary of the tenth-century Samanid court that ruled what is now northeastern Iran

A sixteenth-century painting of worldly and otherworldly drunkenness.

and the area around Bokhara and Samarqand), begins with a lengthy metaphorical description of the preparation of wine and then moves on to a description of a splendid court scene, at which the wine is ceremoniously drunk. This courtly drinking ceremony, called in Persian *bazm,* had its roots in pre-Islamic Iran and was ultimately connected with the religious rituals of the Zoroastrians. The frequent descriptions of *bazm* in medieval and subsequent literature make it clear that the ceremony survived the conquest largely unchanged and was adopted by the Islamic courts that came to rule Iran. A second important survival was the celebration—particularly, but not only, by the court—of the solar festivals, especially those of Nowruz (the vernal equinox) and Mehregan (the autumnal equinox), both of which involved the ritual drinking of wine. Many Persian poems describe the pleasurable festivities associated with these seasonal turning points, and virtually all such descriptions involve enthusiastic invocations to wine. It is noticeable that in such poems much of the vocabulary to do with wine drinking derives from a pre-Islamic Persian vocabulary and is relatively unaffected by the influx of Arabic terms into the language. For example, the most usual words for wine in such poetry are the purely Persian terms *mey* and *badeh,* while those for the vessels from which wine is drunk are the Persian *jam* and *pialeh,* and these words, and many others like them, remained the core poetic vocabulary for the discussion of wine, despite the presence of Arabic equivalents in common use in prose and the spoken language. Among the best-known poems from the early period that center on wine are many by Manuchehri (died 1040) and Farrokhi (died 1037).

Wine in early medieval Persian poetry is associated then with both ritual and pleasure, and the two are seen as mutually supportive; to the Zoroastrians, from which these associations seem to derive, grief was a product of Ahriman, the evil

Above: A gilded Sasanian plate shows a royal drinking ceremony under a vine.

Opposite: The hero Rostam and his king feast and drink wine under a tree bearing clusters of jewels.

principle of the universe, while pleasure and joy were creations of Ahura Mazda, the benevolent principle. To engage in activities that promoted pleasure, and the drinking of wine was prominent among these, was therefore a religiously beneficial act, almost a religious obligation. All this is reflected in the loving descriptions of the celebration of the solar festivals (especially Nowruz) that abound in medieval Persian poetry. The relaxation of taboos and inhibitions, which convivial wine drinking inevitably brings, led to a further association—with flirtation, desire and erotic pleasure. Wine and eros are inextricably linked in Persian poetry, as they have been in the poetries of many cultures.

We can see how these associations play out by glancing at the two most significant Persian poetic narratives completed in the eleventh century, both of which took pre-Islamic stories as their subject matter and therefore inevitably incorporated a number of pre-Islamic cultural presuppositions within their textures. In Ferdowsi's *Shahnameh*, the major epic of Iran, which recounts the pre-Islamic mythology and history of the country, *bazm* is a central concern of the kings and great heroes who dominate the poem: indeed a king's major preoccupations are summed up in the rhyming phrase "*razm o bazm*," with "*razm*" meaning "warfare" ("*o*" means "and"), so that the phrase translates as something like "fighting and feasting" or "battles and banquets." In the mythical stories of the poem's opening the ceremonial and propitious nature of wine drinking at a *bazm* is emphasized (for example a *bazm* is held before the hero Rostam goes off to

rescue the captured Persian warrior Bizhan), and convivial wine drinking of a more informal nature is also the typical relaxation of heroes after victory. A telling example of the association of wine with the hero's life occurs when the poem's greatest hero Rostam is pitted against the Persian crown prince, Esfandyar: the two jockey for position, Esfandyar by pointedly not inviting Rostam to dine with him, Rostam by turning up anyway and then showing his prowess by drinking a vast quantity of wine, which he demands be served undiluted (it seems that the ancient Persians, like the ancient Greeks, normally drank their wine cut with water). The boasting implicit in outdrinking everyone else at a courtly gathering, by imbibing huge quantities of wine, is also the basis of the story of Kebrui, which occurs in the reign of Bahram Gur, told elsewhere in this book (see page 66).

Wine drinking in Ferdowsi is a largely public affair; in Gorgani's *Vis and Ramin*, a romance that is remarkably similar in many of its details to the European tale of *Tristan and Isolde*, this public, courtly element is present, but wine is also emphatically associated with the private, illicit passion of Vis and Ramin for one another, and indeed whenever the lovers are alone the two things they spend almost all their time doing are making love and drinking wine, often simultaneously. The overwhelming effects of passionate love are constantly compared to those of wine, and it is axiomatic in the poem, and in subsequent Persian romances, that the state of mind of a lover is equivalent to the state of mind of someone drunk on wine. One rhyming phrase, a kind of gentler and sweeter echo of Ferdowsi's *"razm o bazm,"* that occurs in *Vis and Ramin*, and occasionally in other poems including a well-known example by Hafez, is *"gol o mol,"* literally "roses and wine"; it is tempting to think that this charming catchphrase is the origin of our "wine and roses" as symbols of a life of fleeting pleasure. (Both words are Persian and pre-Islamic in origin, not Arabic, so the same rhyming association could well have been made in Parthian Persia, where the *Vis and Ramin* story originated, or even before then.)

In the lyrics of Rudaki, Manuchehri and Farrokhi, as in the narratives of Ferdowsi and Gorgani, wine is presented as an integral part of courtly and heroic life, and it is conceived of in almost wholly positive terms. There is no hint at all in Ferdowsi's or Gorgani's work that wine is somehow intrinsically sinful, and this suggestion is relegated to little more than a distant and occasionally registered uneasiness in the works of their lyric predecessors and contemporaries. But of course all these poems were written in an Islamic country, and Islam as we know prohibits wine drinking. Wine drinking was clearly not going to stop in Iran, but it was also equally clearly at odds with orthodox Islamic religious practices. As a result of this rather paradoxical situation, Persian poetry developed in two different directions. First, we find a poetry that celebrated the antinomian and irreligious associations of wine drinking, that mocked orthodox Islamic doctrine and its practitioners, and that made a virtue of deliberately flouting social and religious conventions. The second development was of a poetry that claimed the whole vocabulary and apparatus of wine drinking, but insisted that they were to be read metaphorically—that is, that it was not really about wine drinking at all.

A seventeenth-century picnic at night.

One of the chief models for the deliberately irreligious poems that celebrated wine drinking was, apparently, a genre of Arabic poetry that did just this. The poems of Abu Nuwas (died c. 813), in particular, place two subjects squarely at the center of poetic interest, wine drinking and pederasty, both of which were unequivocally condemned by Islam. Abu Nuwas's mother was Persian, and he lived in Baghdad at a time when the caliphate's capital was undergoing something of a cultural Persianization, and so there may well have been Persian elements in his poetic background; nevertheless it is clear that he drew chiefly on Arab predecessors. It is noticeable, incidentally, that sexual relations in the narrative poems of early medieval Persian are almost always heterosexual in nature and are usually (though not exclusively) between people who are presumed to be more or less social equals; this is so in the *Shahnameh, Vis and Ramin, Varqeh and Golshah,* and various other narratives; this tradition clearly derives from Persian pre-Islamic sources. The short poem tradition however was much more strongly influenced by models in Arabic (such as those by Abu Nuwas) and it is here that we find the theme of pederasty, treated in both literal and allegorical ways, involving what are usually a socially superior older male and a socially inferior younger male. That the theme is common in such poems, but almost unknown in verse obviously deriving from pre-Islamic Persian sources, suggests that this particular topic entered Persian poetry from Arabic poetic convention, rather than from a local Persian tradition. Later the theme spread to narrative verse in Persian too, especially mystically oriented narrative verse, where it is treated allegorically, but it never became as common in narrative verse as in lyric poetry.

Many of the motifs and metaphors Abu Nuwas uses, as well as his poetry's general air of devil-may-care blasphemy, are evident in the work of later Persian poets. As in Abu Nuwas's verse, other frowned-on activities besides wine drinking—such as associating with people of other religions (after the Arab conquest winemaking became the province of Jews, Christians and Zoroastrians, with whom Muslims had perforce to associate if they wished to obtain wine), skepticism as to the exclusive truth of Islam, and engaging in various forbidden sexual practices— also feature prominently in the work of Persian poets active in this genre. The quatrains associated with the name Omar Khayyam (no one knows how many of these quatrains are actually by Khayyam, though the

A sixth-century wine ewer *(zoraq).*

scholarly consensus is "not many") give a good idea of such poetry, as in a more scabrous way do the obscene poems of the fourteenth-century poet Obayd-e Zakani.

More common than such openly blasphemous verse was the kind of poetry that used the language of wine drinking (and often carnal love as well) to talk about religious and specifically Sufi, (mystical) experiences. Sometimes it is clear that this is what is going on, because the poet tells us so, directly or indirectly. The mystical poet 'Eraqi (died 1289), for example, even provides us with a helpful glossary that explains that when he writes "wine" he means "the power of love," that "a wine shop" means "the realm of angels," that "utterly drunk" means "being so absorbed (in God) that one is unconscious of everything else," and so forth. But the explicit pointers 'Eraqi gives are exceptional: Very often we are hard put to say whether a poet means us to read "wine" as "wine," or "wine" as "the power of love," or as something else entirely. Rumi for example is undoubtedly a mystical poet, and presumably 'Eraqi's definitions, or something close to them, can be used to interpret Rumi's verse. But the use of the forbidden intoxications of wine to express the forbidden (or at least suspect to the orthodox) intoxications of mysticism leads to undeniable problems of interpretation. Sometimes one feels that Rumi is talking about real wine; just as, despite the fact that 'Eraqi tells us that when he writes "beloved" he means "God," he ran into real problems when he became too attached to various young men in whom he became interested and once had to skip town when the young man in question turned out to be the governor's son. Sometimes, and perhaps usually, a cigar is just a cigar, a desirable young person is just a desirable young person, and wine is just wine.

The young person motif brings us to the *saqi* or, as the only possible but very infelicitous translation has it, "cupbearer," who features prominently in poems celebrating the drinking of wine, whether these are to be taken literally or as Sufi allegories. The *saqi* is a young individual (almost always male, though it's possible the word was also used for young women), usually a slave, who pours the wine and hands it to the drinker. As with the Greek myth of the handsome youth Ganymede, who performed the same function for the Greek gods and attracted the eye of Zeus, the cupbearer is often a center of erotic attention, and indeed in later Persian poetry the word *saqi* is almost synonymous with "object of desire." We are back with eros and wine, as in Gorgani's *Vis and Ramin*, but the power relations have altered between the individuals involved (Vis and Ramin are presented as virtual equals, the *saqi* is always inferior in status to the drinker) and the frisson of sexual transgression—less strong than it would be nowadays for such a relationship, certainly, but still there—adds to the atmosphere of sometimes rather louche debauchery celebrated in some Anacreontic Persian poems.

The poet who deals most consistently with wine, and whose works have attracted most argument as to their meaning, is undoubtedly Hafez (died 1390). It's clear that Hafez sometimes deliberately writes poems that can be interpreted both literally and allegorically. At other times the feeling of Sufism, the longing for another world where problems are resolved and the speaker is recompensed for earthly sorrow, seems uppermost. Sometimes the literal meaning seems the only plausible one, as when Hafez vehemently complains about a local ruler who forbade the selling of wine and closed the taverns. If the wine in his poems is purely allegorical why should Hafez have cared about this? What is certainly true is that Hafez shows an extraordinary interest in wine, in its various kinds and strengths, in its fermentation, in the different ceremonies and occasions at which it is consumed, in the vessels in which it is stored and from which it is drunk. His wine-related vocabulary probably exceeds that of any other Persian poet. To me, and to many others, this argues a concern with real wine and with everything to do with its production and consumption. It used to be generally thought, and by many still is, that Hafez used the vocabulary of wine and carnal love as allegorical symbols of exclusively mystical concerns. My own feeling is that he is almost always writing about what he says he is writing about, wine and carnal love, and that his occasional hankerings for a more secure and spiritual world, safe from the vicissitudes of earthly life, are just that—occasional hankerings such as might come to anyone who lives long enough and experiences enough of life's reversals and disappointments. But his more usual solace is wine, real wine from his hometown, Shiraz, that remained the center of the area in which Iran's finest wines continued to be made until the Islamic Revolution of 1979 (and, against all odds perhaps, one hopes that it still is).

A *saqi* serving wine in a tree house.

Last night she brought me wine, and sat beside my pillow;
Her hair hung loose, her dress was torn, her face perspired –
She smiled and sang of love, with mischief in her eyes,
And whispering in my ear, she drunkenly inquired:

"My ancient lover, can it be that you're asleep?
The true initiate, when offered wine at night,
Would be a heretic of love if he refused
To take the draught he's given, and drink it with delight."

And as for you, you hypocrites, don't cavil at
Lovers who drain life to the dregs – since we were given
This nature when the world began, and we must drink
The wine that's poured for us, whether from earth or heaven.

So take the laughing wine cup, raise it in your hand,
Caress your lover's curls, and say Hafez has spoken;
How many vows of abstinence the world has seen
So fervently affirmed, and – like Hafez's – broken.

HAFEZ/DAVIS

زلف آشفته و خوی کرده و خندان لب و مست
پیرهن چاک و غزل خوان و صراحی در دست

نرگسش عربده جوی و لبش افسوس کنان
نیم شب دوش به بالین من آمد بنشست

سر فرا گوش من آورد به آواز حزین
گفت ای عاشق دیرینه من خوابت هست

عاشقی را که چنین باده شبگیر دهند
کافر عشق بود گر نشود باده پرست

برو ای زاهد و بر دردکشان خرده مگیر
که ندادند جز این تحفه به ما روز الست

آنچه او ریخت به پیمانه ما نوشیدیم
اگر از خمر بهشت است و گر باده مست

خنده جام می و زلف گره گیر نگار
ای بسا توبه که چون توبه حافظ بشکست

Seventeenth-century painting
by Reza Abbasi, Isfahan.

HOW WINE WAS FIRST FORBIDDEN AND THEN ALLOWED ACCORDING TO FERDOWSI'S *SHAHNAMEH*

At dawn the next morning Bahram called for wine, and his courtiers began another round of merrymaking. At that moment the headman of a village entered with a present of fruit: He brought camel-loads of pomegranates, apples and quinces, and also bouquets of flowers fit for the royal presence. The king welcomed this man, who had the ancient, noble name of Kebrui, and motioned him to a place among the young men there. He handed him a large goblet of wine that held two maund. The visitor was pleased at the king's and his courtiers' attention, and when he had drained the cup, he caught sight of another and felt a craving for it in his heart. In front of all the nobles there he reached out and seized it. He stood and toasted the king, and said, "I'm a wine drinker, and Kebrui is my name. This goblet holds five maund of wine, and I'm going to drain it seven times in front of this assembly. Then I'll go back to my village, and no one will hear any drunken shouts from me." And to the astonishment of the other drinkers there he drained the huge cup seven times.

With the king's permission he left the court, to see how the wine would work in him. As he started back on his journey across the plain, the wine began to take effect. He urged his horse forward, leaving the crowd who were accompanying him behind, and rode to the foothills of a mountain. He dismounted in a sheltered place and went to sleep in the mountain's shadow. A black raven flew down from the mountain and pecked out his eyes as he slept. The group that had been following along behind found him lying dead at the foot of the mountain, with his eyes pecked away and his horse standing nearby at the roadside. His servants, who were part of the group, began wailing and cursed the assembly and the wine.

When Bahram awoke from sleep, one of his companions came to him and said, "Kebrui's bright eyes were pecked out by a raven while he was drunk at the foot of a mountain." The king's face turned pale, and he grieved for Kebrui's fate. Immediately he sent a herald to the palace door to announce: "My lords, all who have glory and intelligence! Wine is forbidden to everyone throughout the world, both noblemen and commoners alike."

A year passed, and wine remained forbidden. No wine was drunk when Bahram assembled his court or when he asked for readings from the books that told of ancient times. And so it was, until a shoemaker's son married a rich, well-born and respectable woman. But the shoemaker's boy's awl was not hard enough for its task, and his mother wept bitterly. She had a little wine hidden away; she brought her son back to her house and said to him,

"Drink seven glasses of this wine, and when
You feel you're ready, go to her again:
You'll break her seal once you two are alone –
A pickax made of felt can't split a stone."

The boy drank seven glasses down, and then an eighth, and the fire of passion flared up in him immediately. The glasses made him bold, and he went home and was able to open the recalcitrant door; then he went back to his parents' house well pleased with himself. It happened that a lion had escaped from the king's lion house and was wandering in the roads. The cobbler's son was so drunk that he couldn't distinguish one thing properly from another; he ran out and sat himself on the roaring lion's back, and hung on by grasping hold of the animal's ears. The lion keeper came running with a chain in one hand and a lariat in the other, and saw the cobbler's son sitting on the lion as unconcernedly as if he were astride a donkey. He ran to the court and told the king what he had seen, which was a sight no one had ever heard of before. The king was astonished and summoned his advisors. He said to them, "Inquire as to what kind of a man this cobbler is." While they were talking, the boy's mother ran in and told the king what had happened.

She said to him, "May you live happily
As long as time endures, your majesty!
This boy of mine's just starting out on life –
He'd found himself a satisfactory wife.
But when the time came…well, his implement
Was just too soft, and he was impotent.
So then I gave the boy (but privately,
To make him father of a family)
Three glasses of good wine; at once his face
Shone with a splendid ruby's radiant grace,
The floppy felt stirred, lifted up its head
And turned into a strong, hard bone instead.
Three drafts of wine gave him his strength and glory
Who would have thought the king would hear the story?"

The king laughed at the old woman's words and said, "This story is not one to hide!" He turned to his chief priest and said, "From now on wine is allowed again. When a man drinks he must choose to drink enough so that he can sit astride a lion without the lion trampling him, but not so much that when he leaves the king's presence a raven will peck his eyes out." Immediately a herald announced at the palace door, "My lords who wear belts made of gold! A man may drink wine as long as he looks to how the matter will end and is aware of his own capacity. When wine leads you to pleasure, see that it does not leave your body weak and incapable."

Ferdowsi/Davis

UNDER A NEW SUN

A rose is still a rose, wherever it might grow,
And wine is always wine, wherever it might flow;
And if the sun should rise up in the western skies
The sun is still the sun, wherever it might rise.

Rumi/Davis

شاخ گل هر جا که میروید گل است
خم می هر جا که می جوشد می است
گر ز مغرب بر زند خورشید سر
عین خورشید است نی چیز دگر

Introducing people to the pleasures of Persian cuisine has been a lifelong passion for me, and I have pondered the connections with wine for many years. But the genesis of this book was pure serendipity.

It happened this way. In 2003 I was invited to a three-day conference in Napa, California, to talk about Persian cooking and give demonstrations. The venue was COPIA, a museum and cultural center whose mission, in its own words, "is to investigate and celebrate the culture of the collective table through wine, food and the arts." Before leaving for California, I received a call from Darioush Khaledi, an Iranian-American like myself. Explaining that he was a sponsor of the COPIA program, he said that he appreciated what I had done in teaching people about Persian food, which is one of the world's oldest and richest culinary traditions yet is only now gaining its rightful recognition in the West. He added that he was in the process of building a Napa Valley winery whose architecture was inspired by Persepolis, the ceremonial capital of the first great Persian empire.

During my stay in Napa, Darioush and his wife, Shahpar (her name is the Persian word for a bird's primary flight feathers), organized a small dinner in a beautiful setting—a tent in the cellar of his half-finished winery, which bore the proprietor's name. (Fittingly enough, Darioush is a version of Darius, the king who built Persepolis.) I loved the look of the building rising around us, admired the

Darioush and Shahpar Khaledi.

wines that had already been made there and found myself wondering how I might address the subject of wine in my own work. At dinner that night, it occurred to me that this place might be the key. It was both a link to the Persian past and a natural extension of it. My new friends told me that they had grown up in Iran, that both of their families had enjoyed wine and that they had always nurtured a dream of making it themselves someday. Now they were living their dream.

But why in the Napa Valley? That question deserves a careful answer, if only because the Khaledis gave it so much thought.

A WINE PARADISE

Located about an hour's drive north of San Francisco, the Napa Valley is narrow—just one to five miles in width—and a little less than thirty miles long. Steep hills, none more than 2,750 feet high, march along either side: the Vaca Range on the east, the Mayacamas Range on the west. Within their embrace, wineries, some of them small affairs and others positively industrial, are everywhere. About 280 of them are strung along the valley's two lengthwise roads, Route 29 and the Silverado Trail, or on the lesser roads that connect those thoroughfares like the rungs of a ladder. Growing grapes and making wines are the main engines of the local economy, but tourism is a major business too. Something like five million people pass through in the course of an average year, sampling wines in the estates' tasting rooms, flocking to the many excellent restaurants (Napa Valley is almost as famous for its food as for its wine) and absorbing the beauty of the area. For sheer pleasantness and sensuous enjoyment, this place is special.

California has many grape-growing locales, together yielding about 90 percent of wine produced in the United States. The Napa Valley accounts for a mere 4 percent of California's output, but that little slice is of exceptional quality, in good part because of the blessings of climate and geology. Most of the valley's rainfall occurs in winter, when it won't harm the growing vines. Summers are moderately hot and dry, softened by morning fog and cooling winds pulled in from the Pacific by the suction effect of hot air rising in California's sun-scorched Central Valley to the east. The combination of warm days and cool nights during the growing season is what some of the finest wine grapes like best.

In addition to the salubrious weather created by its walled-off location between the cool Pacific and the hot interior of California, Napa Valley has a tremendous diversity of soils, the product of a complicated geological past that has included periods of vulcanism, a build-up of sediment, and the protracted shaping of the terrain by the forces of uplift and compression. These processes have endowed the valley with nearly three dozen distinct soil types.

Grapevines, like any plant, are affected by the ground they grow in, and some influence of the soil may be expressed in the wine ultimately made from the vines' fruit. Collectively, Napa Valley winemakers have an exceptionally rich palette of soils to work with, and the results can be striking. Even neighboring estates may produce quite distinctive wines from the same grape varieties.

In the world of wine, the French word terroir is sometimes used to mean the tie between a wine and the soil where its constituent grapes are grown. The term actually has a broader meaning, albeit one that is rather diffuse. Used correctly, it comprises all the different factors that can affect vines at a particular site. Along with soil, these include rainfall, temperature, slope, bedrock, wind, orientation to the sun, and more. Sometimes the meaning of terroir is widened even further to include the human element—the role of grape growers and winemakers in controlling how the qualities of the site find expression in the wine. Whatever the precise usage, there is no arguing with the central point: Place matters.

From the grapes grown in its Napa vineyards—about a hundred acres of vines in total—the Darioush Winery produces a wide range of wines: Chardonnay, Viognier, Cabernet Sauvignon, Shiraz, Merlot and, in some years, a sweet, late-harvest dessert wine made from Sauvignon Blanc and Sémillon grapes and named for the proprietor's wife. (The Darioush offerings also include Pinot Noir, but those grapes are grown in a recently purchased vineyard in the Russian River Valley, in northwest Sonoma County.) Two of the Napa vineyards are located apart from the main property—one on the road between Napa and Yountville, the other on Mount Veeder in the Mayacamas Range. Surrounding the winery itself are thirty-three acres of vineyards, spreading from the valley floor up the slopes of the Vaca foothills behind the winery. The complex is located close to a southern portion of the valley known as the Stags Leap District, a name drawn from tales of stags leaping from outcroppings of the adjacent Vaca Range to escape hunters.

Cabernet Sauvignon

SETBACKS AND TRIUMPHS

The grape-growing virtues of this area have long been obvious. Only a few decades after gold was discovered at Sutter's Mill in 1848 and adventurers and settlers flocked to California, the Napa Valley's first vineyard was established by a man named George Yount. Many other vintners followed, filling the valley with vines by the end of the nineteenth century. But some rough times lay ahead.

The first big setback occurred in the last quarter of the nineteenth century and was shared by grape growers everywhere. Its cause was a tiny aphid called phylloxera, a louse that sucks juices from the roots of susceptible vines, causing them to yellow and die. Phylloxera is native to America, and American grapevine species have evolved defenses against it, but *Vitis vinifera*—the species that produces virtually all of the world's wine—is vulnerable. When some native vines were sent from the United States to Europe to be tested by growers, aphids aboard their roots spread to the vineyards there, with devastating results. Soon phylloxera moved on to vinifera vineyards in Australia, in South Africa and elsewhere. Meanwhile, California shared the agony, because the Eurasian species had been planted there as well.

Eventually the plague was brought under control by planting vineyards with native American rootstocks, which are resistant to phylloxera, and grafting onto them vinifera bud-wood. All viticulture (a term that means the growing of grapevines) now takes this approach, partnering phylloxera-resistant root systems with buds that will generate vinifera canes, leaves and grapes. Phylloxera hasn't vanished as a threat, however. A new and pernicious strain of the pest hit the Napa Valley in the early 1980s and required extensive replanting of vineyards with different rootstocks that could handle it. Viticulture at times resembles an arms race.

The second great calamity to befall the Napa Valley was Prohibition, the ban on all alcoholic beverages in the United States by the Eighteenth Amendment of the Constitution. This measure, the supposed triumph of a temperance movement that had been gathering momentum for decades, took effect in 1920 and was not repealed until 1933. The drinking of alcoholic beverages went on—more extensively than ever, in fact. But it was against the law, giving rise to much smuggling, along with the proliferation of illegal saloons called speakeasies. Winemaking continued too, although it bore little resemblance to the practices of former days. Mostly it was done at home, using inferior, thick-skinned grapes that could be shipped across the country without rotting and readily turned into something with intoxicating properties, but not much else. Meanwhile, many Napa Valley wineries closed, abandoning their precious equipment to the elements.

The nightmare ended eventually, and a new generation of resourceful winemakers set the Napa Valley back on its rightful path in the 1950s and 1960s. Some new approaches were imported, such as the aging of wine in barrels made of French oak, which contributes a distinctive flavor. The matching of grape varieties to growing sites was greatly advanced by research at the Davis campus of the University of California, a center for viticultural and oenological studies. Temperature-controlled stainless steel fermentation tanks were installed in wineries. The men and women in these establishments set their sights high, and they soon enjoyed a triumph that amazed the wine world.

The occasion was a tasting staged in Paris in 1976 by a British wine merchant. It pitted French red and white wines against California wines, all of them in unmarked bottles. The judges included eminent growers from Burgundy and Bordeaux, along with restaurateurs of unimpeachable taste and knowledge. To the astonishment of the tasters, California won the day. A 1973 Stag's Leap from Napa Valley was rated the best Cabernet Sauvignon, beating out a 1970 Château Mouton-Rothschild. Among the Chardonnays, a 1973 Chateau Montelena from Napa was deemed the best, ahead of a Meursault Charmes. Almost instantly, the prices of the best California wines quadrupled. The Napa Valley's capacity to make first-rate wine was now undeniable—confirmed, unexpectedly and somewhat reluctantly, by those millennial masters of winemaking, the French. After that, the valley was the scene of a virtual land rush.

Today, the area is a spectacle of bounty. Vineyards cover the floor of the valley from one side to the other and rise up hillsides toward grassy or tree-clad heights. Sometimes the rows of vines run arrow straight for great distances. On the hills, they may flow sideways along a terraced slope or follow the contours downward in pleasing curves. In every vineyard, the spacing of the rows is maintained to the inch, creating a powerful sense of pattern. Then there are the shifting vineyards' colors, loamy brown in winter, a saturated green in the growing season, yellow in the

Chardonnay

Entrance, fountain and a vineyard
at the Darioush Winery.

autumn. Along the borders of some of the vineyards are silvery-green olive trees
or a sprinkling of bright roses. (The tradition of planting roses near grape vines
is an old one. Both plants are susceptible to powdery mildew, and it has been
said—probably wrongly—that roses will get it first, thus warning of the threat.)
Altogether, the valley is a feast for the eye, immaculately tended, and framed by
the close-pressing Vaca and Mayacamas Ranges.

A VISION OF ANCIENT PERSIA

The Darioush Winery is located on the east side of the Silverado Trail, beyond
some imposing wrought-iron gates and at the end of a long driveway. Glimpsed
for the first time, it seems to have been magically transported here from another
time and place. Its architectural language is drawn in good part from the palace
complex that the Greeks called Persepolis, meaning "city of Persians," built in the
sixth century B.C.E. and looted by Alexander just two centuries later.

Although comparatively modest in scale, the winery makes a stunning
impression. On a broad terrace in front of the entrance are sixteen free-standing
columns, each one eighteen feet high and topped by stylized bulls. The main

building is constructed of travertine stone that was quarried in Iran, not far from the ruins of Persepolis. Pale orange in hue, the stone was shipped to Turkey, where it was cut and given the look of age by a process called tumbling—abrading it with sand in big machines. The building blocks then continued their journey on to the Napa Valley, where they were assembled and given decorative accents modeled on those of the old Achaemenian capital.

Yet the Darioush Winery does not seem mere mimicry. Architect Ardeshir Nozari says, "We wanted to have a kind of dialogue between old and new. This is not a copy." Modern touches are everywhere—in the tall windows, the wrought-iron balconies, the clean lines of the exterior and especially the airy, free-flowing inner spaces. The interior is illuminated by skylights and high-tech German light fixtures. Furniture is by Mies van der Rohe. At the bar where visitors taste Darioush wines, the countertops are made of thick, crazed glass. A kind of illusionistic waterfall extends from the ceiling of the visitors' center down through a stairway leading to the cellars where the wines mature. Water is not actually falling: It slides down vertically strung strands of nylon, its slow-motion descent set agleam by a skylight above.

Persian heritage is evoked by carpets, replicas of ancient drinking vessels in shelves along the walls and, most strikingly of all, by an enormous two-sided

fireplace separating the visitors' area from the administrative quarters of the winery. The fireplace mantels are supported by four life-size bronze statues of Persian warriors, each holding a spear. In cuneiform text engraved on the marble mantels, Darius the Great speaks from a distance of twenty-five centuries:

> *I am Darius, the great king, the king of kings, the king of Persia, the king of the provinces, the son of Hystaspes, the grandson of Arsames, the Achaemenian.*

And:

> *By the favor of Ahuramazda, I am of such sort that I am a friend to right, I am not a friend to wrong. It is not my desire that the weak man should have wrong done to him by the mighty; nor is that my desire, that the mighty man should have wrong done to him by the weak.*

This building's blending of old and new represents a lengthy collaboration between the Khaledis and their Santa Monica-based architects, the Iranian-born husband-and-wife team of Ardeshir and Roshan Nozari. The winery, says Ardeshir Nozari, "is a reminiscence." Bringing it to fruition was a five-year process, from commissioning in 1999 to completion in 2004.

Strong architectural statements are not uncommon in the Napa Valley, and a number of wineries, like Darioush, have a quality of cultural allusion. One early example is the Rhine House, a seventeen-room structure built in 1883 by Frederick Beringer, who came to America from Mainz, Germany, and, with his brother Jacob, ran what is now the oldest continuously operating winery in the valley; Frederick modeled his brick, stucco and redwood residence on his ancestral home in Germany. A very different example is the Sterling Vineyards Winery, a gleaming white structure that might have been transplanted from the Greek island of Mykonos; it was inspired by the valley's Mediterranean climate. And then there is the Robert Mondavi Winery, built in the style of the Spanish missions, where California winemaking began four centuries ago. That an architectural evocation of ancient Persia should appear in this place is not so improbable.

Darioush Khaledi traces his own connection with wine back to early childhood. His father was a military man who made wine at home as a hobby. When he was six years old, he and a younger sister used to dip a cloth into their father's barrels to soak up some of the wine. The two of them then chewed on the cloth, pretending it was candy.

Over the years, his family lived in several cities—Isfahan, Shiraz and Takestan (near Qazvin in Iran)—located in parts of the country where winemaking was a significant part of the economy, although relegated to non-Muslims. Darioush became a civil engineer and went into business with a partner in 1968, at the age of twenty-two. That same year, he married Shahpar, his childhood sweetheart. As his business prospered, he began to collect wine, especially from the great châteaux of Bordeaux. Meanwhile, he deepened his knowledge of wine through books and conversations with like-minded friends. But life in Iran increasingly disturbed him. He had been politically active as a student, committed to the ideal of free speech. In 1976, with the Revolution still three

Replicas of Achaemenian warriors support a mantel inscribed with the words of Darius the Great.

years away but political restraints already tightening, he and Shahpar decided to leave their homeland. They immigrated to America with their two young children, savings of $50,000 and no clear plan about what to do next.

Darioush, entrepreneurial by nature, was soon in rapid motion again. He and his brother-in-law bought a small grocery store in Torrance, California—the start of what would become a supermarket empire. Today, it comprises twenty-three supermarkets spread across southern California, along with extensive real estate holdings.

For some time, this highly successful businessman had been in a position to pursue almost any aspiration. He and Shahpar had often talked about the possibility of making wine, and finally they decided to do it.

Finding the right place wasn't easy. At one point, Darioush almost bought a château in Bordeaux. He also considered properties up and down the California coast. In 1997, after three years of searching, his eye was caught by the Altamura Winery and Vineyards in the Napa Valley. The estate wasn't on the market at the time, but he talked the owner into selling it. Next, he hired a talented winemaker, Steve Devitt, whose commitment to quality equaled his own—and who, by happy chance, had worked at the winery right next door and thus was intimately familiar with local viticultural conditions. The old fieldstone Altamura buildings were torn down to make way for the columned vision that would be the Darioush Winery. Vineyards were replanted to reflect the latest viticultural knowledge about rootstocks, trellising methods, watering systems and so on. A processing system for minimum handling of the grapes was installed.

All winemakers face trade-offs between quality and quantity. For example, vines can be made to produce ten tons of grapes per acre or three tons per acre, depending on how heavily they are watered and fertilized; the greater production usually results in reduced intensity of flavor. Similarly, some vintners get 100 percent of the juice from grapes during crushing; others, seeking a superior wine, opt for gentle crushing and a much lower yield. Quality is affected by innumerable other factors, ranging from the pruning of grape clusters during the growth season to the testing procedures done during and after fermentation.

The Darioush operation is a combination of cutting-edge technology and loving attention to detail, with the focus always on high quality rather than high volume. Shortcuts are verboten, whether in the vineyard or anywhere along the path that turns harvested grapes into wine. Steve Devitt, supervising the process, sees his job in holistic terms. "It's a total concept from vine to wine. You need to know both sides of the equation. You have to experience the entire year of growing grapes in order to make the wine that will be put in the bottle two or three years after that. Our vineyard work is very expensive and involves a tremendous amount of hard labor. Every vine is looked at individually: You may not do to one vine what you do to another vine." The same care is applied when the grapes are ripe in late August and early September. Picking and sorting the clusters is performed by hand; the crushing is done on whole clusters and in small lots. Every step of the fermentation process is closely monitored, and testing and tasting of the wine continues until it is ready for bottling.

THE MAKING OF A WINE

The proprietor at a section of the estate he named for the famous Kholar winemaking district outside Shiraz, Iran.

Consider the creation of a Darioush Shiraz, one of the winery's most celebrated varietals. Here is how Steve Devitt describes the process, starting in the vineyard:

> Shiraz is a vigorous variety and requires a great deal of attention with regard to vine spacing, the training system, the rootstocks, the precise clones grafted to the rootstocks and so on. We have three distinct sites with a total of eight blocks of Shiraz, ranging from 1.2 acres to 5 acres in size. All are planted with rootstocks selected on the basis of soil analysis (minerals, depth, consistency, water-holding capacity, et cetera), the overall climate (rainfall, day-night temperatures, marine influence) and also previous grape-growing observations. Let's look at one block, low in growing vigor because it is very rocky. (Our affectionate name for it is "the rock pile.") Here, the vine rows are spaced seven feet apart and a vine planted every five feet. This adds up to twelve hundred vines per acre. The vines are trained and pruned in a way that will potentially yield forty-eight grape clusters from each vine in an average year.
>
> After pruning and all of the other dormant-season viticulture operations, we pass into spring and summer and the birth of a new vintage. We practice a modified version of sustainable agriculture in all of our vineyards, using a minimum amount of fungicides and planting cover crops to prevent soil erosion. As an aid in growing, we have drip-style irrigation, which is managed according to the needs of each individual row.
>
> Verasion—the term for the change of grape color, from green to red in the case of Shiraz—signals that the year is moving toward harvest. We thin the crop for balance and intensity. Prior to picking, we send out a crew to remove any distressed clusters. Harvest starts at daybreak and continues only as long as the morning stays cool, which aids us later at the winery in controlling the temperature of the crushed fruit. Each cluster is hand-harvested into the picking boxes. As the

Stages in the journey from vineyard to the laboratory where testing is done by winemaker Steve Devitt.

Above: Grapes arriving from the vineyard.

Right: Primary sorting on a moving belt.

Clockwise from top left: Discarded stems from the destemmer; secondary sorting of the destemmed grapes; the crusher; stainless steel fermenting tanks.

pickers advance, a four-person crew sorts the fruit in the field, removing any leaves or other unwanted matter from each box. Then, less than an hour after picking, the boxes are collected and brought to the winery. There, we remove all remaining matter other than grapes, as well as any fruit that is shriveled, rotting or under-ripe. From this point, the fruit goes to a destemming unit that removes the berries from the stems without crushing them. After destemming, the fruit is sorted again to remove any excess stem material or questionable berries. At this point we will partially macerate (crush) the grapes to get 20 to 40 percent of the possible juice. The partially crushed fruit is then directed to the fermenter for cold-soaking at fifty to fifty-five degrees Farenheit, a three- or four-day stage that allows the juice and skins to interact.

The primary, or alcoholic, fermentation lasts from one to two weeks. We use stainless steel fermenters with built-in cooling systems. Several times a day, the juice that separates from the berries and forms a cap on the surface is remixed by either punching it down or pumping the juice over it. This enhances the flavor, aroma and color.

At the conclusion of fermentation, we evaluate the juice and decide between two ways to get still more flavor: either by pressing the skins or macerating the skins in contact with the juice for an extended period of time. Then the juice is drawn off (racked), and the skins are manually shoveled from the fermenters into a press. Like all of our processing, pressing is done gently: How the seeds, skins and other solids are handled can greatly affect final flavors of the wine. The pressed wine will be kept separate throughout the aging period and constantly evaluated to determine an optimal blend for bottling.

The wine is aged in oak barrels bought from French coopers who work with Syrah/Shiraz; they select wood according to our specifications. During the first three months of aging, the second fermentation takes place. In this phase, called malolactic fermentation, bacteria metabolize malic acid to lactic acid, softening the wine. At the conclusion, the wine is racked with air, then returned to the barrel. This aeration may be done additionally to improve the aromatics, color and flavor.

Throughout its aging, the wine is kept at a cellar temperature between 56 and 59°F, with 75 to 80 percent humidity. All lots are kept separate. Each is regularly monitored and evaluated—microbiologically, chemically and sensorily. Every few weeks the wine is topped to minimize overexposure to oxygen, and minimal amounts of sulfur dioxide are applied, which acts as an antioxidant and antibiotic.

Over the sixteen to eighteen months that the individual lots spend in the cellar, we identify those that will be used for our blend. Those not chosen will become Darioush's red table wine. We try out preliminary blends in the lab and evaluate the results through blind tastings, a process of refinement that can last from several weeks to months. When we settle on a final blend, the wine is composed and bottled with the minimum amount of handling.

Thus is a Shiraz made at Darioush. Much more in the way of detail could be added: how the water needs of the vine are determined, how the vine canopy (the leaves) is managed, how ripeness is gauged, what yeasts are used and so on. The point is that Darioush spares no effort in its pursuit of quality. The results, judging from the reactions of both critics and consumers, are superb.

As I mentioned earlier, I met Darioush and Shahpar Khaledi because of my work in the culinary world—specifically, my participation in a conference at COPIA in the summer of 2003. Food brought me to the Napa Valley, and

Tasting to determine the optimum blends.

it has regularly brought me back. In recent years, fifty food writers and guest chefs from around the world have been gathering annually at another eminent Napa Valley establishment, the Culinary Institute of America, whose West Coast branch occupies a former winery called Greystone. Over several days, international cuisines are explored in a series of seminars, tastings and demonstrations for more than five hundred cooks and chefs from around the U.S. These events have been enormously influential in spreading culinary knowledge and showing how ancient food traditions can be applied in a modern context.

I have been lucky enough to represent Persian food there. Each time I participate in this festival of foods and cultures, my senses are excited by new aromas, new tastes and new textures. For my part, I have demonstrated how pomegranates can be seeded in twenty seconds with no mess or bother; how unripe grapes are used as a souring agent; how saffron can be ground with a cube of sugar and diluted in rosewater to bring out the best of its aroma and color; how yogurt and sun-dried yogurt *(kashk)* are used in cooking; how we make golden crust rice in Iran; how to marinate various meat, fowl or fish for delicious kebabs; and much else besides. This information has now spread across America, and the results can be seen both in restaurants and cookbooks everywhere. Like Chinese and Italian food, Persian cuisine is no longer "ethnic food" but is fast becoming an integral part of American cooking.

Meanwhile, a circle has been closed: The Darioush Winery is establishing a world-class kitchen in order to showcase the partnership of food and wine. How that partnership can enrich the pleasures of Persian cuisine is the subject of the rest of this book. As Iranians say when lifting a glass of wine:

"*Nush a nush*" (eternal life, eternal life),

bringing the response,

"*Bash bash*" (may it be so, may it be so).

———— ⬤⬤⬤⬤ ————

Shiraz when spring is here – what pleasure equals this?
With streams to sit by, wine to drink and lips to kiss,
With mingled sounds of drums and lutes and harps and flutes;
Then, with a nice young lover near, Shiraz is bliss.

———————
Jahan Khatun/Davis

شیراز خوش نشر لبت طُعمه در حسن بهار

وآنگه لب جوی ولب جام ولب یار

آواز دف و چنگ و نی و هوی و رباب

اینها همه با نگار کی شیرین کار

I'll buy whatever wine's here, old or new,
And sell the world off gratis when I do:
You ask me where I'm going when I'm dead?
Just bring me wine, and then be off with you!

Khayyam/Davis

PAIRING WINE WITH PERSIAN FOOD

Burke Owens

Persian food, while uniquely different from western European or traditional American cuisine, happily combines the familiar with the exotic. Typical foods found in the Persian pantry include pistachios, pomegranates, limes, saffron, rose petals, orange blossoms, silver angelica, nigella seeds, cumin, cilantro, onion, garlic, rosewater, mint, dill, yogurt, angelica, tarragon, fenugreek, ginger, barberries, walnuts, cherries, dates, fava beans, eggplant, spinach, lamb, chicken, duck, tamarind, cardamom, sumac, rice, chickpeas, lentils, barley, cracked wheat, figs, oranges, grapes, unripe grapes (verjuice) and grape molasses (boiled down grape juice). It is the sophisticated manner in which such ingredients are combined that make this ancient cuisine endlessly fascinating for wine lovers.

Persian dishes are full of contrasts, with a wide variety of flavors ranging from savory to sweet, sharp to mild, and spicy to green. Wines, too, are perceived on the palate in many ways. Acid, tannins, alcohol, sugar, density or weight, and temperature all contribute to this quality, which is roughly equivalent to flavor (not to be confused with aroma). The most important part of successful pairing is to keep in mind the flavor characteristics of wine and foods. There are four ways these two work together:

◆ friendly flavors, which pleasantly agree

◆ mirror flavors, which playfully mimic each other

◆ contrast flavors, which spark off each other, adding interest and complexity

◆ seamless flavors, which mesh perfectly; it's hard to tell where food begins and wine ends

ACIDITY

Acidity is consistently the most important of all flavors in Persian food. Whether from citrus such as bitter orange or lime juice; or from vinegar, verjuice (unripe grape juice) or powdered, unripe grapes; or barberries, pomegranates, sour cherries or tamarind, a refreshingly sharp, even sour flavor profile is typical. This heightened acidity keeps foods inviting and bright—no dull bland flavor profile here. Acidity in food is also one of the best bridges with wine. Make sure, however, that the wine you choose has acidity equal to that of the food or greater. A low-acid wine with a high-acid food will flatten out the wine, making it sweet or bland or even bitter as a result. So do as the Persians do—use verjuice to provide acidity in cooking. The acid flavors in green grape juice are similar to those in a finished wine. In combination they pair seamlessly.

High-acid whites such as Sauvignon Blanc and Riesling or high-acid reds like Pinot Noir, Gamay, Shiraz and Zinfandel are good calls, but any wine with decent, noticeable acidity can work well here. Remember, if you want to work with a less acidic red or white, reduce the tartness of the dish to bring wine and food into balance.

BITTER FOODS

Certain foods—among them fava beans, angelica flowers, orange blossoms and leaves, rose petals, fenugreek, grilled foods, dried lime, quince, saffron and walnut—have bitter flavor qualities, which are used to accentuate a certain astringency or drying character in some Persian dishes. Bitterness in food acts as a seasoning, bringing out earthy flavors and balancing acidity and sweet flavors. Bitterness in wine comes from grape tannins, oak tannins and alcohol, which can taste bitter. Bitterness in both wine and food offer some health benefits, according to recent research studies. So bitter is good, and certainly the combination of Cabernet Sauvignon with a lamb and fava bean braise is a very good example of good taste, good health and good pairing. Look for tannic reds such as Cabernet, Shiraz, Merlot and old-vine Zinfandels or Italian Barolos when pairing bitter foods with wine. A rich, oaky, high-alcohol Chardonnay will also do well.

SWEET FLAVORS

From grape molasses to honey to fruit juice and sugar, Persian food likes the flavor of sweet to contrast with the sour and the bitter. Acidity and bitterness in food often need a touch of sweetness to balance any sharpness or heightened astringency in a dish. Just as with a fine wine, a little fruitiness smooths the rough edges in food. Of course, the wine has to have enough of its own ripeness to stand up to the food to pair successfully. Don't forget that higher alcohol can often make a wine seem sweeter, so a ripe, fruity wine is a great choice with a slightly sweet dish. When enjoying fruity dishes, try Chardonnay or Viognier for white, or a Merlot, Shiraz or Zinfandel for red. But remember: If a dish is actually sweet, a truly sweet late-harvest or fortified wine is the best way to go.

HERBAL NOTES

One of the distinctive qualities of Persian cuisine is an intense "green" character derived from spearmint, dill, Persian basil, tarragon, cilantro, parsley and chives. It gives the food a wild, just-picked freshness and makes for a vivid set of flavors, aromas and colors. The herbal flavors are often accentuated when paired with higher-acid ingredients such as citrus juice, verjuice or vinegar. A green flavor tone opens the way for a number of complex wine interactions. Look for wines with a green edge to match that of the dishes. Among whites, Sauvignon Blanc, Riesling, Chenin Blanc, Gruner Veltliner and cool-climate Chardonnay or Pinot Grigio are all good possibilities. For reds, look for Gamay, Pinot Noir, Grenache, Cabernet Franc, Sangiovese or Zinfandel.

SPICE TONES

Spices are consistently used in Persian food but in a more nuanced way than in, say, some Indian cuisine. They are not employed for shock value or heat but to add a richer framing to key ingredients. Clove, ginger, black pepper, cumin, nigella seeds, cardamom, cinnamon, coriander, turmeric and saffron are all quite popular in varying combinations but rarely as a key flavor. Spice is also popular as an aroma and flavor in many wines, as a result of fermenting or aging wine in new oak barrels. So, as a white to partner with a dish with a distinct spice flavor, look for a toasty Chardonnay or Viognier; for a red, consider an oaky Shiraz, Cabernet Sauvignon, Merlot or Pinot Noir.

OTHER USEFUL GUIDELINES

◆ A rich dish—based on lamb, veal or beef, for instance—is best paired with a rich wine.

◆ A light dish—fish or vegetarian—goes best with a light wine.

◆ A complex dish requires a more complex wine.

◆ A simpler dish is well-served by a simpler wine.

Based on my tastings in Najmieh's kitchen, I have provided brief wine notes about felicitous pairings with the recipes that follow. But these are only suggestions. Many a happy match is made by keeping an open mind and experimenting. The most important rule is this: If it tastes good, then it works.

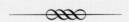

SMALL DISHES AND SALADS

Traditionally, small dishes called *noghl-e mey* in Persian were served with wine after the main meal. In the West, however, we do most of our wine drinking with the meal or at cocktails, and these small dishes are perfect appetizers or hors d'oeuvres. You can either serve one or two of them using the menus I have provided on pages 234–241 or you can make an array of small dishes and serve them at cocktails (and also teas or brunches). I have also included a variety of salads that can be served as one of the courses or on the side of a kebab.

Caviar Canapé
Khaviar

Servings: 2

50 grams Caspian osetra caviar
6 slices of thin toast
1/4 pound butter
1/2 cup pomegranate arils or 1 lime

Caviar is the unfertilized, processed roe of sturgeon. Its name probably comes from the Persian mahi-ye khayehdar, *literally meaning "egg-bearing fish." The best caviar is from the Caspian Sea. There are three main types, each from a different species of sturgeon. The largest eggs, known by the Russian name beluga, are produced by the* fil-mahi, *literally "elephant fish." Beluga sturgeon are on the endangered species list and I don't recommend eating their caviar. The average-sized roe, osetra, comes from* tas-mahi, *or the "bald fish;" and the smallest eggs, sevruga, are those from the* uzun-brun, *or the "long-nosed fish." Besides the size, each type has its own particular flavor. I find osetra to be the tastiest, although sevruga is very good too.*
The most important step in the production of caviar is the salting. The different brands available vary in quality. As long as it comes from the Caspian Sea, it is the real thing, and then it is up to you to decide which type you prefer. An American sturgeon is now being farmed in the U.S. for its roe. Though not as firm or tasty as Caspian caviar, it can be quite good.

I have often been asked, "How does one know if caviar is fresh?" The best answer I can give is that it should smell of the sea but never fishy. Don't keep a jar or can more than a couple of weeks in your refrigerator (never in the freezer). Once opened, you should eat it the same day. Like good wine, the taste starts to get tired after a few hours. Don't use any metallic utensils with caviar, especially silver; metal seems to adversely affect the taste.

Around the Caspian there are various recipes that include the roe of sturgeon. One is with garlic chives in an omelet (the Russians also like to garnish caviar with chopped onions and egg whites). But I believe good-quality caviar should be eaten simply. Place a good-sized dollop on a thin piece of lightly toasted bread and squeeze a little fresh lime juice over it (pomegranate also goes well with caviar).

Serving Note

Serve with toast and butter on a white plate and garnish with pomegranate arils (when in season) or a little lime.

Wine Note

Caviar's delicate, slightly crunchy texture, rich briny flavor and oily finish make it an ideal companion to sparkling wines. Pair with a Blanc de Blanc bubbly. These medium- to full-bodied Chardonnay-based sparklers sweep effortlessly across the palate, cutting the rich salt and oils in the caviar— truly one of the great wine and food pairings in the world. However, if bubbles aren't your thing, try a light dry white such as an Albarino, or a French Sauvignon Blanc such as a Sancerre, or a German Trocken Riesling.

Green Bites: Bread, Cheese, Herbs & Nuts

Dougmaj: Loghmeh-ye sabz-e Eshqabad

Makes: 20 bite-size balls
Preparation time: 10 minutes
Cooking time: none

2 pita breads, cut into 1-inch squares
 (about 2 cups), toasted
1/2 pound crumbled feta goat cheese
4 cups fresh mint leaves or 1/2 cup
 dry mint flakes
1 cup fresh tarragon leaves
1 tablespoon fresh thyme
2 tablespoons dried edible rose
 petals, rinsed
1 cup toasted walnuts or hazelnuts
1/2 cup virgin olive oil or 1/2 cup
 melted butter
20 cucumber slices, 1/4-inch thick
 (long, seedless cucumbers)

Garnish
20 baby basil leaves

No Persian table would be complete without nan-o panir-o sabzi-khordan, *quite simply bread with fresh cheese and fresh greens, herbs and nuts. Here, I am giving you a bite-size, on-the-go, variation adapted from Darioush Khaledi's mother's recipe and a childhood favorite of Darioush's. These are perfect snacks any time, but especially good as a quick breakfast or in the evening with wine.*

Traditionally, cheese, bread and fresh herbs are eaten either as an appetizer, in which small pieces of bread are spread with cheese and garnished with vegetables, herbs, nuts and grapes, or to accompany or conclude the main course. I consider small young fresh sprigs of basil, scallions and radishes to be essential ingredients. Panir, *or cheese, can be any of the cow's or goat's milk cheeses similar to feta cheese, or any soft, white cheese according to your taste.*

1. To make "Green Bites," place all the ingredients except the cucumber slices in a food processor and pulse a few times. Add the olive oil and allow to rest for 1 minute. Pulse again until a grainy paste forms.

2. Gather the paste and divide it into 20 portions (about 1 1/2 tablespoons). Shape each portion into a bite-sized ball.

Serving Note

Place each bite-sized ball on a slice of cucumber and garnish with a baby basil leaf. Arrange on a serving platter.

Wine Note

A very wine-friendly dish. Light- to medium-bodied Sauvignon Blanc or Riesling's herbal aromas and citrusy fruit pair well with the herbs and cut the richness of the cheese. Pinot Noir and Zinfandel are also strong red contenders for this course. For more oomph, a ripe, well-oaked Shiraz pairs nicely with herbs and cheese.

Cracked Wheat & Lentil Bites

Balghur-o adas

Makes: 25 bite-sized balls
Preparation time: 10 minutes.
Cooking time: 55 minutes

3/4 cups brown lentils, pick
 over and rinse
3 cups water
2 teaspoons salt
1 1/4 cups cracked wheat
1 tablespoon ground cumin
1/4 teaspoon ground cinnamon
1 teaspoon ground coriander
1/2 teaspoon fresh ground pepper
1/4 cup virgin olive oil
1 medium onion, peeled and
 thinly diced
2 tomatoes, chopped
1/4 cup verjuice
1 tablespoon grape molasses
2 cups fresh chopped scallions
1 cup fresh chopped flat parsley
1 cup fresh chopped cilantro
25 slices firm tomatoes, 1/4 inch thick
2 heads Boston lettuce, separated and
 washed thoroughly
1 cup basil leaves, thoroughly washed

1. Bring the lentil, water and salt to a boil in a medium saucepan. Reduce heat to medium, cover and cook for 15 minutes. Add the cracked wheat and spices. Cover and cook over medium heat for 15 to 20 minutes or until the wheat and lentils are tender and all the juice has been absorbed.

2. Meanwhile, heat the oil in a deep skillet over medium heat until hot. Add the onion and cook for 15 to 20 minutes until golden brown.

3. Add tomato, verjuice, grape molasses, all the herbs and the lentil mixture. Mix and mash until a grainy paste forms. Adjust seasoning to taste.

4. Divide the paste into 25 portions (about 1 1/2 tablespoons each). Shape each portion into a bite-sized ball.

Serving Note

Place a bite-sized ball on top of a slice of tomato or a piece of lettuce. Place on a serving dish and garnish with a basil leaf.

Wine Note

These small savory snacks combine the nutty lentil, grainy bulgur and green mint with the savory/sweet tomato. Very good with a light, crisp red such as Sangiovese or Tempranillo, or a red blend such as a French Côtes du Rhône.

Pomegranate & Pistachio Meatballs

Kufteh-ye anar-o pesteh

Makes: 20 meatballs
Preparation time: 15 minutes
Cooking time: 15 minutes

1 small onion, peeled and cut into 4
1 cup pistachios or hazelnuts, shelled
1/4 cup bread crumbs
1 cup chopped fresh parsley
1/2 cup chopped fresh tarragon
1 tablespoon fresh lime juice
1 teaspoon red pepper flakes
1 teaspoon freshly ground
  black pepper
1 tablespoon ground cumin
2 teaspoons salt
2 pounds ground lamb or turkey or
  fish fillet (boned and skinned)
1 egg

Glaze
3/4 cup pomegranate paste
1 cup honey or grape molasses
1 cup Pinot Noir wine
1 teaspoon salt
1/2 teaspoon freshly ground black
  pepper
1/2 teaspoon red pepper flakes

Garnish
One package of baby basil, sprouts,
  mint or radishes
1/4 cup fresh pomegranate arils

1. Grind all the ingredients except the meat and egg in a food processor. Transfer to a large mixing bowl and add the meat and egg. Knead with your hands for a few minutes. Cover and place in the refrigerator for 10 to 15 minutes.

2. Preheat the oven to 500°F. Grease a wide, nonreactive baking dish and set aside.

3. Remove the paste from the refrigerator and shape into bite-sized balls (about 1 1/2 tablespoons each). Place the meatballs in the baking dish and brush well with olive oil. Bake in the oven for 5 minutes. Turn the meatballs over once and cook for another 5 minutes.

4. Meanwhile, in a mixing bowl combine all the ingredients for the glaze.

5. Reduce the oven to 400°F. Glaze the meatballs and bake for another 5 minutes to infuse them with the flavor of the wine. Adjust seasoning to taste. If too sour add more honey; if too sweet add more pomegranate paste. Transfer to an ovenproof Pyrex bowl so the meatballs are immersed in the sauce. Keep warm in the oven or a chafing dish until ready to serve.

Serving Note

Place 3 meatballs in the center of a white platter and garnish with baby basil, sprouts, and a few pomegranate arils. For passing these meatballs around with drinks place them in a large serving dish and sprinkle with pomegranate arils and basil. Use toothpicks to pick up.

Wine Note

Not at all like your Naples version of meatballs, these *kufteh* have a wonderful set of sweet and savory flavors. The sour bite of pomegranate combines with honey, zesty herbs, and roasted pistachio and cries out for a medium-bodied, ripe and aromatic Pinot Noir, bringing out the sweetness of the lamb, turkey or fish and the roasted flavors from nuts and sauce. A medium-bodied, ripe and softly tannic Merlot from California is another possibility; it makes the dish richer. Whites will tend to get lost.

Split Pea Patties with Quince

Shami-e lapeh

Servings: 4
Preparation time: 10 minutes
  plus 2 hours refrigeration
Cooking time: 20 minutes

1 pound boned leg of lamb, beef,
  veal or turkey
1 medium onion, peeled and chopped
2 teaspoons salt
1 teaspoon freshly ground pepper
1 teaspoon turmeric
1 pound split peas, pick over and
  rinse
1 teaspoon baking soda, dissolved in
  1 tablespoon water
1/2 teaspoon ground saffron,
  dissolved in 2 tablespoons hot water
3 eggs
2 cups oil or more, for frying

Garnish
Quince paste (1/4 pound, or use
  recipe below) or 1/2 cup grape
  molasses
1/2 pound goat cheese
Fresh basil, edible flowers, such as
  roses or marigolds, and lavash bread

Servings: 6
Preparation time: 15 minutes
Cooking time: 5 hours, or more at
  room temperature to dry out

3 pounds quinces (about 5 medium
  quinces)
1 3/4 cups sugar or grape molasses
1 tablespoon fresh lime juice
1 teaspoon ground cardamom
  (optional)
2 packages (3 ounces each) Certo
  liquid pectin; mix with 3/4 cups
  water and bring to a boil, whisking
  until there are no lumps.

Garnish
1 cup ground pistachios (optional)

1. In a medium saucepan combine the meat, onion, 1 1/2 teaspoons of salt, pepper, turmeric and 2 cups of water; cover and cook over medium heat for 45 minutes or until tender. Remove from the heat and drain (reserve the juice to use later on if the meat is too dry). Puree the meat in the food processor and transfer it to a large mixing bowl.

2. In another medium-sized saucepan, bring to a boil the yellow split peas in 4 cups water with 1/2 teaspoon salt. Reduce heat, cover and cook for 30 minutes or until tender. Drain and reserve the juice. In the same food processor puree the split peas and transfer into the mixing bowl.

3. Add the baking soda and saffron to the mixing bowl. Add the eggs one by one and knead for a few minutes, until a soft paste is created. If it is too dry, add some of the reserved juices. Cover and refrigerate for 2 to 24 hours.

4. Place a bowl of warm water next to your cooking pan. With damp hands, separate the meat paste into lumps the size of walnuts. Flatten each lump between your palms into a round shape and press a hole in the center with your finger; this helps to cook the inside of the patties.

5. In a large skillet, heat 1 cup of oil over medium-low heat until hot (but not smoking), then fry the patties on each side for about 5 minutes, until golden brown, adding more oil if necessary. There should be enough oil so that the patties are half immersed in oil. Drain and set aside.

Quince Paste

1. Wash and rub the fuzz off the quinces. Core, grate and place in a large nonstick pot. Cover (do not add water) and cook over low heat for 1 hour, stirring occasionally with a rubber spatula.

2. Prepare an 8-inch square pan by rinsing and lining the bottom and all sides of the moist pan with plastic wrap, or use a disposable plastic container with cover.

3. Add the sugar and lime juice. Cover and simmer over low heat for 2 1/2 hours, stirring occasionally with a rubber spatula, until tender. The quinces' color should change to dark pink.

4. Puree the quince in a food processor and return to the pot. Add cardamom and pectin. Cook over medium heat for 10 minutes, stirring constantly with a rubber spatula. You should have a thick, reddish paste. To test, drop a teaspoon of paste on a chilled plate. The paste should remain firm and not run. If the paste runs, continue to cook until it passes the test. Remove from heat.

5. Transfer the quince paste to the prepared pan. Pack it firmly with a spoon and garnish with ground pistachios. Cool in room temperature for at least 2 hours then cover and chill in refrigerator for 2-24 hours.

Serving Note

Arrange 3 hot patties on an individual plate, garnish with a slice of quince paste, a slice of goat cheese, sprigs of basil and mint, a radish and a piece of warm, thin lavash bread on the side. Serve hot or cold as an appetizer or as a small dish *(noghl-e mey)* with wine.

Wine Note

Savory with a hint of sweetness, these patties require a rich wine—whether white or red. Pair with Chardonnay or Merlot.

Fava Beans with Angelica

Baqala pokhteh

Servings: 4
Preparation time: 1 minute
Cooking time: 15 minutes

2 pounds fresh fava beans in the pod,
  or 1 pound frozen fava beans
1/4 cup salt
1/4 cup red wine vinegar
2 teaspoons angelica powder and/or
  seeds
1/2 teaspoon cayenne pepper
  (optional)

Note
You can also cook the fava beans in
the traditional Persian style: fresh in
the pod, and shell them as you eat
them. This is similar to the way the
Japanese eat edamame.

1. Rinse the fresh beans and shell them from the pod. Frozen beans are already shelled.

2. In a large pot, bring 5 quarts of water and 1/4 cup of salt to a boil.

3. Add the fresh beans and boil briskly for 10 to 15 minutes. (For frozen beans, add them to the boiling salt water mixture and boil for 5 minutes or until tender.)

Serving Note

Drain the beans, transfer a portion to a plate, sprinkle with the vinegar, angelica powder and cayenne pepper. Garnish with sprigs of fresh herbs and serve.

> *Bring wine, my boy – I'm dying now I know,*
> *Blind-drunk is how I'll quit this earthly show;*
> *I entered life completely ignorant*
> *And that's precisely how I plan to go.*
>
> Faghani/Davis

ساقی قدحی که از میان خواهم رفت

آشفته و مست از جهان خواهم رفت

در آمدنم نبود از هیچ خبر

آن دم که رو نیز چنان خواهم رفت

Wine Note

A pungent, slightly bitter flavor makes this dish a challenge for most whites—
though a ripe Viognier or Gewurztraminer might pull it off. So pair with a
Zinfandel or Shiraz—big reds with structure to handle the flavors.

Vine Leaf Wrapped Lamb Kebab

Kabab-e barg-e mo ba shireh-ye angur

Servings: 6
Preparation time: 40 minutes
Cooking time: 6 minutes

Kebab
2 pounds twice-ground lamb (or beef
  with extra fat, chicken thighs or
  boneless fish fillets as alternatives)
2 teaspoons coarse salt
1 teaspoon freshly ground black
  pepper
1/2 teaspoon baking soda
2 small onions, peeled and finely
  grated
2 cloves garlic, peeled and grated
1 inch fresh ginger, gated
1 teaspoon ground cumin
1 1/2 teaspoons ground coriander
1 teaspoon hot curry powder

Wrap
50 fresh grape leaves in season or
  1 jar (16 ounces) of canned leaves
  packed in brine
1/2 cup olive or peanut oil
1 cup unripe grapes: iffresh, remove
  stems; if in brine, drain

Garnish
1 package (12 ounce) of lavash bread
1/2 cup grape molasses
1 pound red grapes
1 cup fresh basil leaves
1/2 cup drained yogurt *(labneh)*

Skewers
18 wood skewers soaked in water for
  at least 30 minutes

1. If you are using fresh grape leaves, pick small and tender ones. Blanch, drain and rinse. For canned grape leaves, drain in a colander.

2. In a mixing bowl, combine the lamb and the rest of the kebab ingredients. Knead with your hands for about 2 minutes to form a paste. Cover and let stand for 15 minutes at room temperature.

3. Using damp hands, divide the meat paste into 16 equal lumps about the size of a walnut. Roll each into a sausage shape 4 inches long.

4. Place one layer of grape leaves, vein side up, on a flat working area and nip off the stems. Place a portion of meat on the narrow end of the leaves. Fold over the sides and roll up the leaves into a meat package.

5. Thread the meat package on a skewer. On the same skewer thread 2 unripe grapes and paint the package and the unripe grapes generously with oil. Place on an oiled baking sheet. Repeat for all the meat portions. Cover and keep in a cool place until ready to cook.

6. Grill the kebabs gently for 2 to 3 minutes on each side. Serve hot, or keep warm in the oven or a chafing dish until ready to serve.

Serving Note

Spread a layer of lavash bread or vine leaves on a warm plate and place 3 skewers of kebabs on top. Pour grape molasses over the kebabs. Garnish with fresh red grapes, fresh basil leaves, and a dollop of drained yogurt. Serve as an appetizer.

Wine Note

Pair with an aromatic white such as Viognier or a red such as Pinot Noir. These scented wines add their own perfume to the kebabs, making for an off-the-charts combination (a very good example of how the Persian flavor palate is extremely wine friendly). Smoky, meaty, zesty and slightly sweet and sour—a perfect match with wine.

Grilled Eggplant with Sun-Dried Yogurt, Dates & Mint Fries

Kashk-e bademjan

Servings: 4
Preparation time: 50 minutes
Cooking time: 1 hour 10 minutes

3 medium eggplants or 6 Chinese or
  10 Italian eggplants
1/2 cup extra virgin olive oil
3 large onions, peeled and thinly
  sliced
10 cloves garlic, peeled and crushed
1 teaspoon turmeric
2 tablespoons dried mint flakes
1 teaspoon salt
1/4 teaspoon freshly ground black
  pepper
1/2 cup liquid sun-dried yogurt
  (kashk), whisked with 1/2 cup water

Garnish *(N'ana daq)*
1 tablespoon oil
4 tablespoons dried mint flakes
1/4 teaspoon turmeric
1 cup walnuts, toasted and chopped
1 cup sun-dried yogurt *(kashk)*
1/4 teaspoon ground saffron,
  dissolved in 1 tablespoon hot water
1 cup pitted dates, sliced or 1 cup
  grape molasses
Toasted flat bread
Fresh basil leaves

1. Peel the eggplants and cut them first into four lengthwise slices and then into halves (4-by-2-inch slices). To remove any bitterness, soak the eggplants in a large container of cold water with 2 tablespoons salt. Let stand for 20 minutes. Rinse with cold water and blot dry.

2. Brush the eggplant slices on all sides with 4 tablespoons of oil. Grill them on all sides on a nonstick baking sheet. Drain and set aside.

3. Preheat the oven to 350°F.

4. Heat 4 tablespoons oil and golden-brown the onion and garlic. Remove from heat and add the turmeric, mint flakes, salt and pepper, stirring well. Set aside.

5. In a nonreactive, wide, ovenproof baking dish place alternating layers of eggplant and the onion and garlic mixture, pouring the diluted sun-dried yogurt all over between each layer. Cover, and bake in the oven for about 40 minutes.

6. Adjust seasoning to taste. Cover and keep warm in the oven until ready to serve.

7. To make the garnish, heat 1 tablespoon of oil in a small skillet. Add the mint flakes and turmeric, remove from the heat and stir well. Set aside.

Serving Note

For individual servings: place a few eggplant slices in the center of each dish and top with a little sun-dried yogurt *(kashk)*. Add a little mint and a drop of saffron on top of the sun-dried yogurt. Sprinkle with a few toasted walnuts and a few dates. Serve with bread and fresh herbs (a bowl of fresh basil, for example). Serve as an appetizer or as a small dish *(noghl-e mey)* with wine.

Wine Note

Savory, tangy and a little bit fruity, this is another unusual combination of flavors that was made to pair with wine. It has enough stuffing to stand up to red wines such as a medium to full-bodied, ripe Shiraz but can also work with richer whites such as rich but dry Viognier. The grape molasses seamlessly ties the wine and food flavors together.

Herb Kuku with Barberries

Kuku-ye sabzi

Makes: 50 bite-sized pieces
Preparation time: 20 minutes
Cooking time: 30 minutes

12 eggs
1 teaspoon baking powder
2 teaspoons advieh (Persian spice
  mix)
2 teaspoons salt
1 teaspoon freshly ground black
  pepper
4 cloves garlic, peeled and crushed
2 cups finely chopped fresh garlic
  chives or scallions
2 cups finely chopped fresh parsley
2 cups finely chopped fresh coriander
  leaves
2 cups chopped fresh dill
1 tablespoon dried fenugreek leaves
2 tablespoons all-purpose flour
1/2 cup olive oil for baking
Parchment or baking paper

Garnish
1/2 cup dried barberries
2 tablespoons oil
1 teaspoon sugar
1 cup toasted walnuts
1 package (12 ounce) of lavash bread

Yogurt Garlic Sauce
2 cups *labneh* or plain drained yogurt
2 cloves garlic, peeled and grated
1 teaspoon dried mint (optional)
1/2 teaspoon salt
1/2 teaspoon freshly ground pepper
1 teaspoon dried organic rose petals
  (optional)

This fresh herb kuku is traditionally Iranian but popular from Erzurum in Turkey to Samarqand in Uzbekistan. In Iran it is eaten on New Year's Day (the festival of Nowruz, at the spring equinox): The green of the herbs symbolizes rebirth, while the eggs represent fertility and happiness for the year to come.

1. Preheat the oven to 400°F.

2. Break the eggs into a large bowl. Add the baking powder, advieh, salt and pepper. Lightly beat with a fork. Add the garlic, chopped herbs, fenugreek and flour. Mix thoroughly but do not overmix because egg whites separate from the rest of the ingredients during cooking.

3. Oil a baking sheet and line it with baking paper. Oil the baking paper with 1/2 cup of oil. Pour in the egg mixture and bake uncovered for 30 minutes.

4. Remove the baking sheet from the oven, allow to cool and cut the kuku into 2-by-3-inch strips.

5. Pick over and soak the barberries in cold water for 10 minutes, drain in a sieve, rinse and set aside. Heat 2 tablespoons oil in a medium-sized nonstick skillet over medium heat, add the barberries and 1 teaspoon sugar and stir-fry for 20 seconds (the barberries can burn easily; be careful).

6. To make the yogurt garlic sauce, combine all the ingredients for the sauce in a mixing bowl.

erving Note

Arrange a few pieces of the kuku on an individual serving dish, garnish with a tablespoon of barberries and a dollop of yogurt sauce, and add a few toasted walnuts and a piece of bread on the side.

Wine Note

Eggs work with most wines—the herbs lead one to Sauvignon Blanc, Riesling or Gruner Veltliner. A light bitterness from the mix of fenugreek, cilantro and dill makes a great match with aromatic whites.

Cauliflower Kuku

Kuku-ye gol-e kalam

1. Preheat the oven to 400°F.

2. Heat 1/4 cup of oil in a large skillet over low heat. Add the onion and stir-fry for 5 minutes until translucent. Add the garlic, cauliflower, salt, pepper, cumin, turmeric, chili and parsley, and stir-fry for 5 to 10 minutes until the cauliflower is soft. Allow to cool.

3. Break the eggs into a mixing bowl, add the baking powder, flour, milk and cheese, and whisk lightly.

4. Add the stir-fried ingredients to the egg mixture and mix lightly.

5. Transfer to six generously oiled 6-inch-diameter, nonstick pans. Bake in the preheated oven for 20 to 25 minutes, until firm. Remove from the oven and place on a wet surface, cover with a kitchen towel and allow to cool for 5 minutes. To unmold the kuku, loosen the edges with a rubber spatula and turn each pan, one at a time, quickly onto a baking sheet (tap slightly if necessary to unmold). Keep warm uncovered in the oven until ready to serve.

Serving Note

Serve warm or cold with yogurt and flat bread. Garnish with herbs.

Wine Note

Once again, eggs and wine are a good mix. The richness of cauliflower and cheese lead to Chardonnay—or Merlot if a red is preferred.

Servings: 6
Preparation time: 20 minutes
Cooking time: 25 minutes

1/2 cup vegetable oil, butter or ghee
1 small red onion, peeled and thinly sliced
2 cloves garlic, peeled and crushed
1 small head cauliflower or 1 pound frozen florets, coarsely chopped
1 1/2 teaspoons salt
1/2 teaspoon freshly ground black pepper
1 teaspoon ground cumin
1/4 teaspoon turmeric
1 green bird chili, chopped, or 1/4 teaspoon cayenne
1/2 cup chopped fresh parsley or cilantro
6 eggs
1/2 teaspoon baking powder
1 tablespoon flour or bread crumbs
1/2 cup milk, or soy milk
1/2 cup Parmesan cheese, grated, or goat cheese, crumbled (if using goat cheese, reduce salt to 1 teaspoon)

Lamb Liver Kebab

Kabab-e jigar

1. Clean the liver and cut into strips 1 inch thick.

2. Light a bed of charcoal and let it burn until the coals glow evenly, or preheat the grill or broiler.

3. Skewer strips of liver onto 2/3-inch-wide skewers.

4. Grill over hot coals for approximately 4 minutes. Turn them frequently. Sprinkle with pepper, lime juice and coarse salt.

Serving Note

Serve immediately hot on the skewer, on bread, with spring onions, basil and pickled garlic (see page 204).

Wine Note

The rich, concentrated flavors of the lamb liver will pair quite well with a full-bodied white such as Chardonnay or an aromatic red like Pinot Noir.

Servings: 4
Preparation time: 5 minutes
Cooking time: 4 minutes

1 lamb liver (1 1/2 pounds)
1/4 teaspoon freshly ground black pepper
Juice of 3 limes or 1/2 cup verjuice
1 teaspoon coarse salt

Garnish
1 package (12-ounce) lavash bread
1 bunch spring onions
1 cup basil leaves
1 cup pickled garlic

Note
Lamb liver is smaller and tastier than calf liver (though you can subsitute the latter). Lamb liver is harder to find, but it can be ordered from specialty butchers.

Spicy Lamb Turnover

Sanbouseh or *Navaleh* or *Mantou*

Makes: 16 pieces
Preparation time: 1 hour plus
  3 hours for dough to rise
Cooking time: 35 minutes

Homemade Dough
2 egg yolks
1 cup plain yogurt
1 cup corn oil
2 1/2 cups all-purpose flour, sifted
  with 1 teaspoon baking powder

Filling
1/2 cup oil, butter, or ghee
1 onion, peeled and finely chopped
4 cloves garlic, peeled and crushed
1 pound ground lamb, chicken or fish
1 Napa cabbage head, shredded and
  sprinkled with 2 teaspoons salt; let
  stand for 15 minutes then squeeze
  out the liquid
2 teaspoons salt
1 teaspoon grape molasses
2 teaspoons cinnamon
1/2 teaspoon ground cloves
1/2 inch fresh ginger root, peeled and
  shredded
1 teaspoon coriander
2 teaspoons ground cumin
1/2 teaspoon cayenne
1 teaspoon freshly ground pepper
1 cup chopped fresh cilantro
1 cup chopped scallions

Glaze
1 egg, lightly beaten with 2
  tablespoons milk

Dip
1 cup wine vinegar
1 cup grape molasses

You can make these turnovers using a homemade dough or ready-made puff pastry. If you choose to fry your turnovers however, you can use ready-made large-sized pot sticker wrappers available in oriental groceries and some supermarkets.

1. In a mixing bowl, use a mixer or food processor to beat the egg yolks until creamy. Add yogurt and oil. Gradually blend in 2 1/2 cups of the sifted flour mixture. Knead well to produce a dough that does not stick to your hands (add more flour if necessary). Place the dough in a plastic bag and refrigerate for 3 hours. Remove the dough from the plastic bag and roll the dough on a floured surface until it is 1/8 inch thick.

2. Meanwhile, prepare the filling by heating the oil in a large skillet over medium heat. Add the onion and stir-fry for 10 minutes. Add the garlic and meat and fry for another 20 minutes, until the meat is completely dry. Add the remaining ingredients and stir-fry for another 5 minutes. Adjust seasoning to taste. Remove from heat and allow to cool.

3. Heat the oven to 350°F.

4. On a cool, lightly floured work surface knead and spread out the dough. Cut out small circles 3 1/2 inches in diameter, using the open end of a glass dipped in flour or a floured cookie cutter. Fill each circle with 1/2 teaspoon of the filling. Fold each circle to a crescent shape and, using a fork, press the dough around the filling to seal it.

5. Carefully transfer the crescent shapes one by one onto a baking sheet lined with a baking mat. Do not crowd. Paint the *sanbouseh*s with the glaze.

6. Bake in the preheated oven until golden brown, about 30 to 35 minutes.

Serving Note

Place 3 *sanbouseh*s on a serving plate. Beside it, place a small bowl of the vinegar and grape molasses dipping sauce. Garnish with fresh herbs. Serve hot.

Wine Note

Spices play a big role in this dish, especially sweet spices that mimic the flavors of oak found in many red wines. So pair with Merlot, Cabernet Sauvignon or Shiraz—all will work well.

Spinach Yogurt Salad

Borani-e esfenaj

Servings: 4
Preparation time: 10 minutes plus
  15 minutes refrigeration
Cooking time: 30 minutes

2 tablespoons vegetable oil,
  butter or ghee
2 onions, peeled and thinly sliced
2 cloves garlic, peeled and crushed
5 cups fresh spinach, washed and
  chopped, or 1 packet (about 12
  ounces) frozen, thawed
1 1/2 cups drained yogurt
1/2 teaspoon salt
1/2 teaspoon freshly ground black
  pepper

Garnish (Optional)
1/2 teaspoon ground saffron threads,
  dissolved in 2 tablespoons hot water
1 tablespoon dried rose petals

I like to serve three of the following four yogurt salads in small bowls together on a platter and call them "three yogurts" seh mast.

1. In a large skillet, heat the oil over medium heat. Add the onions and garlic and fry for 20 minutes, stirring occasionally to prevent burning, until the onions are soft and brown.

2. Add the spinach, cover and steam for 5 to 10 minutes, until the spinach is wilted.

3. Remove from heat and let cool for 10 to 15 minutes; transfer to a mixing bowl.

4. Add the yogurt, salt and pepper. Refrigerate for at least 15 minutes, or up to 8 hours.

Serving Note

Place about 1/2 a cup of the borani on a plate and garnish with saffron water and rose petals, or any other edible flower, and serve with some slices of crisp flatbread.

Servings: 6
Preparation time: 10 minutes
Cooking time: 2 hours 55 minutes

2 1/2 cups dried white broad beans,
  picked over and rinsed, or cooked
  white beans in a jar
6 cups water
2 teaspoons salt
1/2 cup virgin olive oil
1 small red onion, diced
2 cloves garlic, crushed and chopped
1/4 cup fresh lime juice or verjuice
1 tablespoon grape molasses
1 cup chopped fresh dill weed
1 1/2 cups drained yogurt

White Broad Bean Yogurt Salad

Borani-e lubia sefid

1. In a medium saucepan, bring the beans, water and salt to a boil. Reduce heat to medium, cover and cook for 2 1/4 hours, until the beans are tender and all the water has been absorbed. Remove from heat, drain and allow to cool. Or use already cooked white beans.

2. Heat the oil in a skillet over medium heat. Add the onion and garlic, stir-fry for 2 minutes, until the onion is lightly golden brown. Add the lime juice and grape molasses. Remove from heat and set aside.

3. In a large mixing bowl whisk the dill and the yogurt. Add the beans and onion mixture. Toss well. Adjust seasoning to taste.

Serving Note

Place a portion on an individual serving platter and serve with bread.

Cucumber & Yogurt with Mint & Rose Petal Salad

Borani-e khiar

Servings: 4
**Preparation time: 15 minutes
  plus 1 hour refrigeration**

1 long seedless cucumber or 3
  pickling cucumbers, peeled and
  sliced
3 cups plain whole yogurt
1 tablespoon chopped fresh mint
2 tablespoons chopped fresh dill
  weed
2 cloves garlic, peeled and grated
1 teaspoon salt
1/4 teaspoon ground pepper

Garnish
1 tablespoon dried rose petals
1/2 teaspoon chopped fresh or
  dried mint

In a serving bowl, combine all the ingredients. Toss thoroughly and season to taste with salt and pepper.

Serving Note

Chill in refrigerator for 1 hour before serving. Transfer to a serving dish and garnish with dried rose petals and mint.

Wine Note

Light and refreshing—perfect with a light, dry Riesling from Germany or the Finger Lakes of New York State.

Servings: 4
Preparation time: 15 minutes
Cooking time: 1 hour

4 large eggplants
4 cloves garlic, peeled and grated
1 teaspoon salt
1/4 teaspoon freshly ground black
  pepper
1 teaspoon ground cumin
1/4 teaspoon cayenne powder
1 cup drained yogurt
1 tablespoon chopped fresh mint
1/4 teaspoon saffron, dissolved in 1
  tablespoon hot water

Variation
Replace yogurt with 1/4 cup verjuice
or vinegar, and 1 cup chopped,
toasted walnuts.

Eggplant Yogurt Salad

Borani-e bademjan

1. Preheat oven to 350°F. Wash eggplants and prick in several places with a fork to prevent bursting. Place whole eggplants on oven rack and bake for 1 hour. Be sure to put a tray under the eggplants to catch drips.

2. Remove from oven and allow to cool. Peel, remove seeds and mash the eggplants. Transfer to a mixing bowl. Add the grated garlic, salt, pepper, cumin and cayenne, and mix with yogurt. Adjust seasoning.

3. Transfer to a serving dish and garnish with mint and saffron water.

Serving Note

Place the eggplant dish on a platter. Cut up toasted lavash bread and arrange around the dish on the platter. Serve as an appetizer.

Wine Note

Creamy, bright and tangy—pair with a glass of Chardonnay or Pinot Gris.

Beet & Grape Molasses Salad

Labu ba shireh-ye angur

Servings: 2
Preparation time: 5 minutes
Cooking time: 1 hour 10 minutes
  if fresh beets are used

2 large uncooked beets or 1 can (16
  ounces) cooked beets, drained
2 cloves garlic, peeled and sliced
1 tablespoon chopped fresh mint or 1
  teaspoon dried mint
1 tablespoon grape molasses (more
  or less depending on the sweetness
  of the beets)
1/4 pound feta goat cheese (optional)

1. If using fresh beets, place the beets with the skins in a baking dish, add 1 cup water, cover and bake in a preheated 350°F oven for about 1 hour or until tender.

2. Peel and cut the beets into 3/4-inch cubes.

3. In a medium-sized skillet, heat 2 tablespoons oil over medium heat, add garlic and stir-fry until golden brown. Remove from the heat. Add mint, grape molasses and the beets. Stir well.

Serving Note

Transfer to a serving dish and garnish with fresh mint and some goat cheese.

Wine Note

Beets, with their root vegetable texture and sweetness, combine well with many red wines. Cabernet Sauvignon, Merlot, Shiraz and even Pinot Noir can work well here. If the beets are nice and sweet, use a less tannic red such as a medium- to full-bodied, ripe Shiraz, or a Pinot. But if the beets are earthy, go for Cabernet or Merlot.

Pomegranate & Angelica

Anar-e daneh shodeh ba golpar va namak

Servings: 4
Preparation time: 2 minutes

2 cups fresh pomegranate arils (about
  2 pomegranates)
1 teaspoon angelica petals
1 teaspoon coarse salt

Pomegranates are delicious served with wine before and after a meal.

To seed a pomegranate, slice off the crown with a sharp knife and make a superficial spiral cut in the skin around it. Press both thumbs into the open crown and pull the fruit apart. Hold each half, seed side down, over a nonreactive bowl and tap the skin with a heavy spatula to dislodge the seeds from the membrane that holds them.

Serving Note

Seed pomegranates and serve fresh. Sprinkle with ground angelica petals *(golpar)* and coarse salt.

Wine Note

First you taste the sharp sweet bite of the fruit, then a slight bitter floral character from the angelica and finally a little salt to soothe the palate. Is there a wine to pair with this exotic combination? Yes! For a white go with a floral, juicy Viognier that combines stone fruit flavors and pretty honeysuckle aromas. The red to pour is a medium- to full-bodied, ripe Shiraz—meaty, oaky and supple in texture, made to pair with the crisp fruit, bitter flowers and savory salt. A rich Blanc de Noirs Champagne with a touch of age or oak will also work very well indeed.

Caspian Olive Tapenade

Zeytoun parvardeh

Servings: 4
Preparation time: 15 minutes
Cooking time: none

1 cup walnuts, toasted
5 cloves garlic, peeled
1 cup fresh mint or 1 tablespoon
  dried mint
1 cup chopped fresh cilantro
1 tablespoon chopped fresh oregano
  or 1/8 teaspoon dried oregano
1 tablespoon angelica powder *(golpar)*
1/2 teaspoon salt
1/4 teaspoon freshly ground pepper
1/2 jalapeño pepper, seeded and
  diced (optional)
1 teaspoon ground cumin (optional)
1 teaspoon grape molasses or honey
1/4 cup olive oil
1/2 cup fresh pomegranate juice
1 pound green pitted olives

Garnish
1 tablespoon walnuts, toasted and
  chopped
1/4 cup pomegranate arils
1/2 cup pitted green olives
3 sprigs cilantro

Place all the ingredients in a food processor and pulse until you have a chunky paste. Transfer to a mixing bowl, toss well and adjust seasoning to taste. Cover and refrigerate for 15 minutes and up to 3 days.

erving Note

Place in a serving bowl. Garnish with walnuts, fresh pomegranate arils, whole olives and cilantro. Serve with toasted bread cut into 4-inch pieces.

ine Note

Rich and concentrated, this tapenade style spread is made for red wines. The combination of herbs, nuts and especially the pomegranate gives it a tannic-like character that will pair well with a ripe, spicy red Zinfandel (below 15% alcohol) or Shiraz or even a weightier Pinot Noir.

Four-Hearts Green Salad

Salad-e chahar maghz

Servings: 4
Preparation time: 5 minutes
Cooking time: 5 minutes

4 romaine lettuce hearts
1 tablespoon honey or grape
  molasses
1/4 cup almonds
1/4 cup pistachios
1/4 cup hazelnuts

Dressing
1 tablespoon mustard
2 tablespoons sherry vinegar
1/2 cup olive oil
1/2 teaspoon salt
1/2 teaspoon freshly ground pepper

1. Thoroughly wash the lettuce. Pat dry and keep cool.

2. In a nonstick skillet, heat the honey. Add the nuts, stirring constantly with a rubber spatula until lightly caramelized. Set aside.

3. To make the vinaigrette, whisk the mustard and vinegar in a mixing bowl. Gradually add the olive oil while whisking until smooth and creamy. Add salt and pepper and adjust seasoning to taste.

erving Note

Just before serving, toss the lettuce, nuts and vinaigrette. Serve in the center of individual plates.

ine Note

The romaine hearts, combined with the candied nuts and a sweet vinaigrette, make a surprisingly good match with red wines. The dressing is not too sharp and so the meaty almonds and pistachios take center stage. Very good with both Pinot Noir and a medium- to full-bodied, ripe Cabernet Sauvignon.

Servings: 4
Preparation time: 15 minutes

1 firm ripe tomato
1 long seedless or 5 Persian
  cucumbers
2 scallions, chopped
3 radishes, sliced
1/2 cup chopped fresh parsley
1 tablespoon chopped fresh mint
1 tablespoon chopped fresh coriander

Dressing
4 tablespoons olive oil
1 tablespoon lime juice
1 tablespoon verjuice
1 clove garlic, peeled and crushed
1 teaspoon salt
1/4 teaspoon freshly ground
  black pepper

Garnish
1 package (12 ounces) lavash bread
Edible flowers
Basil sprouts

Servings: 4
Preparation time: 25 minutes
Cooking time: none

1 small red onion, peeled and diced
1 cup pitted olives
2 long seedless cucumbers, or 6
  pickling cucumbers, peeled and
  thinly sliced
2 medium pomegranates, seeded
  (2 cups)

Dressing
1 clove garlic, peeled and crushed
1 tablespoon lime juice
1 tablespoon pomegranate paste
1/4 teaspoon red hot pepper flakes or
  1/4 teaspoon chili paste
2 teaspoons grape molasses or honey
2 teaspoons toasted sesame oil
1 teaspoon salt
1/2 teaspoon freshly ground black
  pepper
1/2 cup olive oil
4 cups shredded greens, frisée,
  arugula or romaine lettuce

Garnish
1/2 cup walnuts, toasted and coarsely
  chopped
1/2 cup feta cheese, crumbled

Shirazi-Style Cucumber & Tomato Salad

Salad-e shirazi

1. Drop the tomato into scalding hot water. Remove immediately and rinse under cold water, peel and cut into 1/4-inch cubes (traditional), or in slices as in the photograph.

2. Peel and cut cucumber into 1/4-inch cubes (traditional), or in slices as in the photograph.

3. Place all the vegetables and herbs in a salad bowl, cover and keep chilled.

4. In a mixing bowl, whisk together the olive oil, lime juice, verjuice, garlic, salt and pepper. Adjust seasoning to taste and set aside.

erving Note

Just before serving, pour the salad dressing over the salad and toss well. Place a piece of crisp lavash bread, big enough to cover the plate, in the center of an individual plate and place a portion of the salad on top. Garnish with edible flowers and sprouts.

ine Note

Tomatoes are often surprisingly wine friendly—it just depends on how you prepare them. Shirazi-style combines the crisp cucumber with the meaty tomato and adds a splash of tangy verjuice—delicious with a glass of light- to medium-bodied red such as a Pinot Noir.

Tribal Cucumber Salad

Salad-e anar-o khiar

1. Combine the onion, olives, cucumber and pomegranate arils in a mixing bowl and set aside.

2. To make the salad dressing, thoroughly mix all the salad dressing ingredients.

erving Note

Just before serving, pour the dressing over the salad, toss well and adjust seasoning to taste. Serve individually on a bed of greens and garnish with walnuts and cheese.

ine Note

This flavorful mix of onion, pomegranate, cucumber and olives is so tasty it's addictive. The tangy fruit and sweet/sour dressing just begs for a good Pinot Noir.

Peach Salad

Salad-e Hulu

Servings: 4
Preparation time: 15 minutes

1 frisée lettuce, stem removed and
  chopped into 4-inch pieces
5 firm peaches, washed and sliced
  (1/8s)
2 scallions, washed and sliced
1 cup chopped fresh mint or dill
  leaves

Dressing
2 tablespoons verjuice or fresh lime
  juice
2 tablespoons rice vinegar
1/4 cup olive oil
2 tablespoons walnut oil
1/2 teaspoon salt
1/4 teaspoon freshly ground pepper
1/4 cup caramelized walnuts
  (optional, recipe below)

1. Thoroughly wash the lettuce. Pat dry and keep cool.

2. In a glass mixing bowl, place the sliced peaches, scallions and mint, and sprinkle with verjuice to prevent from discoloring. Set aside.

3. Just before serving, add the vinegar, olive oil, walnut oil, salt and pepper to the peaches. Add the lettuce and toss gently. Adjust seasoning to taste.

Serving Note

Place a portion in the center of a serving plate and garnish with caramelized walnuts.

Wine Note

This is one of those surprising combinations that work as a salad course but could also jump over to dessert, especially at the height of peach season. Pair with a sweet late-harvest wine for dessert such as Sauternes or with a dry Gewurztraminer for a savory salad.

Makes: 2 cups
Preparation time: 5 minutes
Cooking time: 15 minutes

2 cups shelled walnut halves
1/4 cup grape molasses

Walnuts Caramelized with Grape Molasses

Gerdu-ye sukteh ba shireh-ye angur

1. Heat the walnuts in a wide skillet over medium heat, shaking the skillet frequently, for 5 to 15 minutes until they are toasted. Do not walk away; the walnuts will burn easily.

2. Line a baking sheet with parchment paper.

3. Reduce heat to very low and add the molasses, shaking and swirling the skillet for 2 to 3 minutes until the syrup covers all the nuts.

4. Remove from heat and spread over the parchment paper. Allow to cool thoroughly. Store in a jar and use as needed.

Eggplant Salad

Naz khatun

Servings: 4
Preparation time: 15 minutes
Cooking time: 10 minutes

4 Chinese eggplants (about 2
 pounds), cut into 3-by-1-inch strips
1/2 cup grape seed oil*
1 medium onion, peeled and diced
2 cloves garlic, peeled and crushed
2 medium tomatoes, peeled and
 chopped
2 tablespoons pomegranate paste
1/4 cup verjuice
1 teaspoon salt
1/2 teaspoon freshly ground black
 pepper
1 teaspoon angelica powder
1/2 cup chopped fresh mint leaves or
 2 teaspoons dried mint
1 teaspoon toasted sesame oil
1 teaspoon grape molasses

Garnish
2 cups baby garlic, mint or basil
 sprouts

* Grape seed oil is good for high-heat
cooking and stir-frying, and has a
neutral flavor.

1. Cut the eggplants into 3-by-1-inch strips. To remove bitterness, place the eggplants in a large container of cold water with 2 tablespoons salt; allow to rest for 20 minutes. Drain and blot dry.

2. In a large skillet, heat 1/2 cup oil until hot, but not smoking, and deep-fry the eggplants until golden brown and tender. Remove the eggplants with a slotted spoon and transfer to a large nonreactive mixing bowl. Set aside.

3. In the same skillet, heat the remaining oil over medium heat. Add the onions and garlic, and stir-fry for 20 seconds. Add the tomatoes, pomegranate paste and verjuice, and stir-fry for another 20 seconds. Remove from heat.

4. Add the tomato mixture to the eggplant in the mixing bowl. Add salt, pepper, angelica powder, mint, sesame oil and grape molasses. Toss gently and adjust seasoning to taste.

Serving Note

Place a portion of eggplant mixture in the center of individual plates on a bed of sprouts. Serve warm or cold with rice and/or pan-roasted quail (see page 171), or other meat or fish according to your fancy. This recipe may be made up to 4 hours in advance. If the salad is refrigerated for more than an hour, remove it from the refrigerator 10 minutes before serving.

Wine Note

The heftiest of all these salads, the eggplant is smoky, contrasting with the pomegranate fruit. Pair with a white wine such as rich but dry Chardonnay to bring out the sesame notes, or choose a medium- to full-bodied, ripe Cabernet Sauvignon for greater depth and richness if you prefer red.

SOUPS

I have given you seven soups that cover all the seasons. They can be served in large portions with plenty of bread as meals unto themselves, or you can serve them in smaller portions to start a meal.

A sixteenth-century miniature depicts outdoor preparations for a noodle soup.

Chilled Yogurt Soup with Rose Petals & Raisins

Abdugh khiar ba tilit

Servings: 6
Preparation time: 15 minutes
Cooking time: none

Croutons
1 large whole wheat pita bread, cut
   into 1/2-inch squares

Garnish
1 cup raisins
3 tablespoons fresh mint leaves
1 tablespoon dried rose petals, rinsed
   thoroughly with cold water

Soup
3 cups plain whole or low-fat yogurt
2 cloves garlic, crushed, peeled and
   finely chopped
2 teaspoons coarse salt
1 teaspoon freshly ground black
   pepper
1 cup chilled water

Cucumber-Walnut Mixture
1 long seedless cucumber or 4
   pickling cucumbers, peeled and
   diced
1/4 cup chopped spring onions
2 tablespoons chopped fresh mint
2 tablespoons chopped fresh dill
2 tablespoons chopped fresh oregano
   or 1/2 teaspoon dried oregano
1 tablespoon chopped fresh thyme or
   1/2 teaspoon dried thyme
4 tablespoons chopped fresh tarragon
   or 1 tablespoon dried tarragon
1/2 cup raisins
1/4 cup shelled walnuts, coarsely
   chopped

1. Cut pita bread into 1/2-inch crouton squares. Spread in a baking dish and toast under broiler for a few minutes. Transfer to a serving bowl and set aside.

2. To make the garnish, place the rose petals in a small plastic container, add the mint, the raisins and 1/4 cup of cold water, and mix. Cover and place in the freezer for 2 hours. This helps to perfume the raisins and soften the rose petals. If you are feeling particularly adventurous you can place this mix in ice cube containers to freeze it and then use the ice cubes in the soup.

3. Combine the yogurt, garlic, salt and pepper, and mix thoroughly with 1 cup of chilled water. Stir well and adjust seasoning to taste.

4. Combine the cucumber, spring onions, mint, dill, oregano, thyme, tarragon, raisins and walnuts in a nonreactive bowl, cover and keep chilled.

Serving Note

Just before serving, put 2 tablespoons of the cucumber mixture into individual serving bowls and pour the yogurt mixture over it. Add 3 ice cubes, the raisins and mint garnish and serve. Pass around the croutons so people can serve themselves according to their taste.

Wine Note

Creamy and just short of sweet, this cooling summer-style soup could work as an appetizer, light lunch or even a dessert. Pair it with a lush dry wine like Viognier or a late-harvest wine like Semillon or Riesling. The dry wine tames the richness while the sweet wines make it as lush as you like.

Pomegranate Soup

Ash-e anar

Servings: 6
Preparation time: 20 minutes
Cooking time: 1 hour 15 minutes

4 tablespoons vegetable oil
2 teaspoons cumin seeds
2 large onions, peeled and thinly
  sliced
2 cloves garlic, crushed and peeled
2/3 cup mung beans
4 cups chicken broth or water
1/2 cup short-grain rice, picked over
  & rinsed
4 cups pomegranate juice or 1 cup
  pomegranate paste diluted in 4 cups
  water
2 1/2 teaspoons coarse salt
1 teaspoon freshly ground
  black pepper
1/4 teaspoon ground cinnamon
1 tablespoon grape molasses
  (shireh-ye angur)
1 tablespoon angelica powder
1 pound baby spinach, washed and
  drained
1 cup chopped fresh dill
1 cup chopped fresh parsley
1 cup chopped fresh mint leaves, or
  2 teaspoons dried mint

Garnish
1 tablespoon vegetable oil
2 cloves garlic, mashed and chopped
1/4 teaspoon turmeric
1/2 cup chopped fresh mint or 1
  tablespoon dried mint flakes
1 cup pomegranate arils (about 1
  large pomegranate—optional)
1/2 cup toasted, coarsely chopped
  walnuts

Note
This soup can also be prepared by
cooking all the ingredients except for
the herbs. Add the herbs just before
serving to achieve a fresh look as
shown in the photograph.

1. Heat 4 tablespoons oil in a medium-sized, nonreactive, heavy-bottom pot over medium heat. Add the cumin and stir-fry for 20 seconds until aromatic. Keep a cover handy to prevent the cumin from jumping out of the pot. Add the onion and garlic, and stir-fry for 10 minutes. Add mung beans and stir-fry for 3 minutes longer. Add the broth and bring to a boil. Reduce heat, cover and simmer over medium heat for 20 minutes. Add rice and simmer over medium heat for another 20 minutes.

2. Stir in the pomegranate juice, salt, pepper, cinnamon, grape molasses, angelica powder, spinach, dill, parsley and mint. Bring back to a boil, reduce heat and simmer over low heat for 30 minutes. Use a hand-held mixer and partially puree the ingredients.

3. Adjust seasoning to taste; the soup should be sweet and sour. Cover and keep warm until ready to serve.

4. To make the garnish, heat 1 tablespoon oil in a skillet, add garlic and stir-fry for 1 minute or until golden. Add turmeric and stir-fry for 20 seconds. Remove from the heat, add the mint, stir and set aside.

Serving Note

Pour the soup into individual soup bowls and garnish with the garlic-mint mixture, pomegranate arils and walnuts.

Wine Note

This soup, with all the sweet, sour, astringent character of fresh pomegranate, but combined with chicken stock, grains and spinach, is sublime. While amazingly flavorful on its own, it hits it off nicely with Pinot Noir or with a five-year-old Sercial or Rainwater-style Madeira from Portugal. Lots of zing in these matches; definitely not for shy palates.

Pistachio Soup

Sup-e pesteh

Servings: 6
Preparation time: 10 minutes
Cooking time: 35 minutes

Garnish
1 tablespoon vegetable oil
1 cup shelled pistachios
1/2 cup barberries, rinsed
1 teaspoon grape molasses

Soup
1 cup unsalted pistachios, shelled
6 to 8 cups chicken broth or water
1 tablespoon vegetable oil, butter or
  ghee
2 tablespoons cumin seeds
1 teaspoon coriander seeds
1/2 teaspoon fresh ginger, grated
1 Thai bird chili, chopped, or 1/4
  teaspoon cayenne pepper
1 small onion, thinly sliced
2 leeks (white and green parts),
  chopped
2 cloves garlic, peeled and chopped
1 cup rice flour
1 teaspoon salt
1/4 teaspoon turmeric
1 teaspoon freshly ground
  black pepper
1 cup Seville orange juice, or 3/4
  cup fresh orange juice mixed with
  1/4 cup fresh lime juice, or 3/4 cup
  verjuice

1. To prepare the garnish, heat 1 tablespoon oil in a heavy-base, medium-sized pot over medium heat. Add 1/2 cup shelled whole pistachios, 1/2 cup barberries and 1 teaspoon grape molasses, and stir-fry for 20 seconds (barberries can burn easily; be careful). Use a slotted spoon to transfer the mixture from the pot to a small bowl. Set aside.

2. Grind the pistachios in a food processor or grinder. Add 2 cups broth and continue to grind until you have a smooth, creamy pistachio puree. Set aside.

3. In the same pot used earlier, heat 1 tablespoon oil until very hot. Add the cumin and coriander, and cook for 10 seconds until the seeds stop crackling (keep a lid handy to avoid losing seeds that can fly out). Add the ginger, chili, onion, leeks and garlic. Cover and allow to stew gently for 5 minutes. Add the rice flour, the pistachio puree, 4 cups of broth, salt, turmeric and pepper. Whisk constantly and bring to a boil.

4. Reduce heat, cover and simmer over very low heat for 30 minutes, stirring occasionally. Add more broth if the soup is too thick for your taste.

5. Just before serving, add the Seville orange juice and adjust seasoning to taste. Cover and keep warm until ready to serve.

Serving Note

Place 1 tablespoon of garnish in each of six warm soup bowls and pour in 1 ladle full of soup. Serve with crisp hot bread.

Wine Note

An amazing set of flavors and textures are found in this pale, creamy soup. The pistachio spice really comes through, combining with the barberry garnish to balance the rich soup. White wine is best here—a Pinot Gris or a Viognier can stand up to this soup yet not overwhelm it.

Barley & Leek Soup

Ash-e jow

Servings: 6
Preparation time: 20 minutes
Cooking time: 2 hours

2 tablespoons vegetable oil, butter
  or ghee
2 onions, peeled and sliced
2 cloves garlic, peeled and crushed
1 carrot, peeled and chopped
3 leeks, washed thoroughly and
  chopped (white and green)
8 to 10 cups chicken or beef broth
1/2 cup barley
1 teaspoon salt
1 teaspoon freshly ground black
  pepper
1 1/2 cups sour cream
1/4 cup verjuice or juice of 1 lime
1 teaspoon sugar or grape molasses
1/2 cup chopped fresh cilantro
1/2 cup chopped fresh tarragon
1/2 cup chopped fresh dill

Garnish
2 tablespoons chopped fresh parsley
1/2 teaspoon freshly ground black
  pepper

1. In a large pot, heat the oil over medium heat. Add the onions and garlic and fry for 15 minutes, stirring occasionally, until golden brown. Add the carrot and leeks, and stir-fry for 1 minute.

2. Add the broth, barley, salt and pepper. Bring to a boil, reduce the heat to low, cover and simmer stirring occasionally for 1 hour, or until the barley is tender.

3. Using a slotted spoon, transfer the solid ingredients to a blender. Add the sour cream, verjuice, sugar and the fresh herbs. Blend thoroughly. Return the puree to the pot and stir constantly with a wooden spoon for 1 minute, until the soup begins to boil. Reduce heat and correct seasoning to taste, adding salt, pepper or verjuice as needed. Cover and keep warm until ready to serve.

Note
You may make this soup a day in advance, which can help the flavors blend. Store it in the refrigerator and reheat it just before serving.

Serving Note

Pour the soup into individual, warm serving bowls and garnish with fresh parsley or oregano, and pepper.

Wine Note

The verjuice, onion and herbs give this soup an exotic flavor that is delicious with small sips of a crisp Manzanilla Sherry or a big, bold Chardonnay.

Bulgur & Sun-Dried Yogurt Soup

Ash-e balghur

Servings: 6
Preparation time: 20 minutes
Cooking time: 1 hour 10 minutes

1/2 cup vegetable oil
2 large onions, peeled and thinly
 sliced
2 cloves garlic, crushed, peeled and
 chopped
1 teaspoon turmeric
2 tablespoons dried mint flakes
1 teaspoon salt
1 teaspoon freshly ground black
 pepper
1 cup mung beans, picked over and
 thoroughly rinsed
10 to 12 cups chicken broth or water
1/2 cup ground walnuts
3/4 cup wheat bulgur (cracked wheat)
1 cup chopped fresh parsley
1 cup chopped fresh cilantro
1 cup chopped fresh dill
2 cups chopped fresh spinach
1 1/2 cups sun-dried yogurt *(kashk)* in
 liquid form
1/4 cup verjuice (unripe grape juice)
 or 2 tablespoons lime juice

Garnish
1 cup chopped fresh dill weed
1/4 cup drained yogurt

1. Heat the oil in a Dutch oven over medium heat, add the onions and fry for 15 minutes until golden brown. Add garlic, turmeric, mint flakes, salt and pepper, and stir-fry for 20 seconds.

2. Add the mung beans and broth, and bring to a boil. Reduce heat to medium and simmer, covered, for 15 minutes, stirring occasionally. Add the walnuts and bulgur, bring back to a boil and cook covered over medium-low heat for 20 minutes until the beans are tender.

3. Add the herbs and continue to cook partially covered for another 15 minutes.

4. Use a hand-held mixer and partially puree the soup.

5. Reduce heat to very low and gradually add the sun-dried yogurt, stirring constantly for 5 minutes to prevent curdling. Add verjuice.
Adjust seasoning to taste, adding more salt or verjuice if necessary.
Add more broth if the soup is too thick for your taste. Cover and keep warm on very low heat until ready to serve.

Serving Note

Pour the soup into a serving bowl and garnish with fresh chopped dill and a dollop of yogurt.

Wine Note

The flavors here are intense yet very balanced with a long, earthy, tart finish. A dry, chilled Manzanilla Sherry cuts the richness and balances the sharp notes with its own crisp bite. If you prefer red, look for a medium- to full-bodied, ripe Shiraz or Zinfandel. Their spice tones will bring out even more flavor in the soup.

Noodle Soup with Verjuice

Ash-e reshteh

Servings: 6
Preparation time: 20 minutes
Cooking time: 2 hours

Soup
1/2 cup vegetable oil
4 large onions, peeled and thinly sliced
10 cloves garlic, peeled and crushed
2 teaspoons salt
1 teaspoon freshly ground pepper
1 teaspoon turmeric
1/4 cup dried chickpeas, picked over and rinsed
1/2 cup dried kidney beans, picked over and rinsed
10 to 12 cups beef or chicken broth or water
1/2 cup dried lentils, picked over and rinsed
1/2 pound Persian noodles or dried linguine, broken in half
1 tablespoon unbleached flour, dissolved in 2 cups water
1/2 cup coarsely chopped fresh chives or scallions
1/2 cup chopped fresh dill
1 cup chopped fresh parsley
1 pound washed and chopped fresh spinach or 1 pound frozen spinach, thawed and chopped
1 cup sun-dried yogurt *(kashk)*
1/4 cup verjuice

Garnish *(Nana daq)*
2 tablespoons vegetable oil
2 cloves garlic, peeled and crushed
2 tablespoons dried mint flakes, crushed
1/2 teaspoon turmeric

Note
This soup can also be prepared by cooking all the ingredients except the herbs, which can be added just before serving, as shown in the photograph.

You may make this soup, which is associated with the Persian New Year, a day in advance so that the flavors can blend. Store it in the refrigerator and reheat it just before serving. To prepare the fresh herbs, soak them in a large bowl of lukewarm water for 10 minutes. Drain in a large mesh colander, rinse grit from the bowl, return the herbs to the bowl and cover with water again. Immediately drain in the colander. Repeat the quick soak and drain twice. Then dry the herbs (with a salad spinner or paper towels) and chop them.

1. Put the oil into a 2 1/2-quart pot and set the pot over medium heat. Let the oil warm for 1 minute or 2, then add the onions and stir-fry for 10 minutes with a long-handled spoon. Add the garlic, salt, pepper, turmeric, chickpeas and kidney beans. Stir-fry for another minute.

2. Pour in 10 cups of broth and bring the mixture to a boil. Then reduce the heat to medium, cover the pot and simmer for 45 minutes.

3. Add the lentils. Cover the pot and cook for 20 more minutes.

4. Add the noodles and cook, uncovered, for 10 minutes, stirring occasionally.

5. Add the dissolved flour, chives, dill, parsley and spinach, and continue to cook for 30 minutes, or until the beans in the soup are tender.

6. The soup should be the consistency of a good chicken noodle soup; if it is too thick, stir in warmed stock or water. Now either let the soup cool and refrigerate it (if you are making it a day ahead) or reduce the heat to very low, cover the pot and keep the soup warm while you make the garnish (if you are going to serve the soup immediately).

7. To make the garnish, heat 2 tablespoons of vegetable oil in a small skillet set over medium heat. Add the crushed garlic and stir-fry for 1 minute, until the garlic pieces turn golden brown. Remove the skillet from the heat, stir in the mint and turmeric, and set aside.

8. When you are ready to serve the soup, remove it from the heat, add the yogurt and verjuice, and stir for 5 minutes with the long-handled spoon. Taste the soup and add salt if it is needed.

Serving Note

Serve the soup in individual bowls and decorate with the garnish.

Wine Note

A fresh New Year's soup like this relies on the bright, herbal and earthy bean and lentil notes. Zesty and moderately rich, pair with an aromatic wine such as Riesling, Albarino or, best of all, a citrusy Sauvignon Blanc.

Tamarind & Kholrabi Soup

Ash-e nargil-o tamr-e hendi

Servings: 6
Preparation time: 20 minutes
Cooking time: 1 hour 10 minutes

4 tablespoons vegetable oil, butter or
 ghee
2 teaspoons black mustard seeds
1 teaspoon fenugreek seeds
1 onion, peeled and thinly sliced
1 tablespoon curry powder
2 hot green chilies, seeded and
 chopped
1 pound kohlrabi or butternut squash,
 peeled and diced (1-inch cubes)
1 cup red lentils
6 to 8 cups chicken broth or water
2 teaspoons salt
1/2 teaspoon freshly ground black
 pepper
2 cups coconut milk
1/2 cup rice flour, diluted in 2 cups
 water
2 tablespoons tamarind paste
2 tablespoons grape molasses
2 cups chopped fresh cilantro leaves

1. Heat the oil in a heavy-based, medium-sized saucepan over medium heat until very hot. Add the mustard seeds and fenugreek seeds, and cook for 10 seconds until aromatic or the seeds stop crackling (keep a lid handy to stop seeds from flying out). Add the onion and stir-fry for 5 minutes. Add the curry powder, chili, kohlrabi and red lentils and stir-fry for another minute. Add 6 cups broth, salt and pepper, and bring to a boil. Cover and simmer for 40 minutes until the kohlrabi is tender. Add more broth if the soup is too thick for you.

2. Use a hand-held mixer to partially puree the soup. Add the coconut milk, diluted rice flour, tamarind and grape molasses, and stir constantly. Bring back to a boil. Reduce heat to low, cover and simmer over low heat for 15 minutes, stirring occasionally.

3. Adjust seasoning to taste.

Serving Note

Just before serving, place a little cilantro in each of 6 warm soup bowls and pour in a ladle full of soup.

Wine Note

A sharp set of flavors with the astringent tamarind balances the rich coconut. Big, full-bodied whites such as Viognier, Chardonnay or Pinot Gris have enough flavor to work. Or consider a fortified wine such as Sercial or Rainwater-Madeira—with enough acidity there to cut the rich soup while adding their own delicate notes.

MAIN COURSES

Saffron Steamed Rice with Golden Crust

Chelow ba tah dig

Servings: 6
Preparation time: 15 minutes
Cooking time: 1 hour 10 minutes

4 cups long-grain basmati rice
8 cups water
2 tablespoons salt
2 cardamom pods
1/4 cup rosewater
2 tablespoons plain yogurt
1 cup butter or vegetable oil or ghee
1 teaspoon ground saffron, dissolved
  in 1/4 cup hot water
1 teaspoon cumin or nigella seeds
  (optional)

Saffron Water:
Ground saffron threads with 1 cube
of sugar until transformed into
powder. In a glass container dissolve
1 teaspoon ground saffron in 1/4 cup
of hot water or, for a distinctive flavor,
rosewater.

Rice without the Crust
Eliminate step 6. In step 7, steam the
rice for 30 minutes over medium heat.

Reheating Leftover Rice
Place the rice in a nonstick pot with
1/2 cup water, cover tightly and place
over low heat for 15 to 20 minutes.

Cooking Brown Rice
In step 2 boil the rice for 30 minutes
instead of 6 to 10 minutes.

1. Pick over the rice. Basmati rice like any other old rice contains many small solid particles. This grit must be removed by picking over the rice carefully by hand. Wash the rice by placing it in a large container and covering it with warm water. Agitate gently with your hand, then pour off the water. Repeat 5 times until the rice is completely clean. Thoroughly washed rice gives off a delightful perfume when cooked that unwashed rice does not. If using long-grain American or Texmati rice, it is not necessary to wash 5 times; once will suffice. Drain and set aside.

2. In a large nonstick pot, bring 8 cups of water with the salt, cardamom and rosewater to a boil. Pour the washed and drained rice into the pot. Boil briskly for 6 to 10 minutes, gently stirring twice with a rubber spatula to loosen any grains that may have stuck to the bottom. When the rice rises to the surface and feels soft, it is ready. Drain rice in a large, fine-mesh colander and rinse with 2 or 3 cups of cold water.

3. In a bowl, mix 3 spatulas of rice, 2 tablespoons yogurt, 3/4 cup butter, 1/2 cup water, a few drops of dissolved saffron water and the cumin seeds.

4. Spread the yogurt-rice mixture over the bottom of the nonstick pot and pack down. This will help to create a tender golden crust *(tah dig)*.

5. Take one spatula full of drained rice at a time and gently place it on top of the yogurt and rice mixture, gradually shaping the rice into a pyramid. This shape leaves room for the rice to expand and enlarge. Poke one or two holes in the rice pyramid with the handle of a wooden spatula.

6. Cover and cook rice for 10 to 15 minutes, or until steam rises, over medium-high heat in order to help form a golden crust.

7. Dissolve the remaining butter in 1/2 cup hot water and pour over the rice pyramid. Place a clean dish towel or 2 layers of paper towels over the pot and cover firmly with the lid to prevent steam from escaping. Cook for 50 minutes longer over medium-low heat.

8. Remove the pot from heat. To help free the crust from the bottom of the pot, allow the pot to cool on a damp surface for 5 minutes without uncovering it. There are two ways to serve the rice. The first is to hold the serving platter tightly over the uncovered pot and invert the two together, unmolding the entire mound onto the platter. The rice will emerge as a golden crusted cake. Serve in wedges. The second way is to put 2 tablespoons of rice in a dish, mix with remaining saffron water and set aside for garnish. Gently, taking one spatula full of rice at a time, place the rice on a serving platter without disturbing the crust. Mound the rice into a cone. Sprinkle the saffron rice garnish over the top. Detach the layer of crust, either whole or in parts, from the bottom using a wooden spatula and place on a platter. Serve either on the side or arrange the pieces of crust around the rice.

Individual Rice Crusts *Tah dig-e mast-e fardi*

1.) Use 6-inch-diameter nonstick pans, or large muffin pans.

2.) Preheat oven to 500°F.

3.) In each pan, place 2 tablespoons melted butter, 2 tablespoons yogurt, 1 tablespoon water, a drop of saffron water, a pinch of salt and pepper. Mix well with a rubber spatula until creamy. Spread the yogurt mixture evenly on the bottom of the pan. Fill each pan with parboiled rice from step 2 on the facing page. Pour a tablespoon of melted butter, a tablespoon water and a drop of saffron water over the top of the rice.

4.) Cover the entire pan with a piece of oiled aluminum foil. **Press down** over the aluminum foil and seal tightly so that steam cannot escape. Bake for 45 minutes in the preheated 500°F oven.

5.) Remove the pan from the oven and place it on a damp dish towel for 1 minute without uncovering to allow it to cool. To unmold the rice, uncover and loosen the edges with a rubber spatula, then cover the pan with a baking sheet and, holding the baking sheet and mold together, turn them upside down. The rice in the pan should unmold itself onto the baking sheet. Keep warm uncovered in the oven until ready to serve.

Individual Potato Rice Crusts *Tah dig-e sib zamini-e fardi*

Use the instructions above but eliminate the yogurt and replace it with sliced potatoes. Cut 1/4-inch-thick rounds of Idaho russet potatoes, 4 per pan. Do not cut the potatoes too thinly or they will burn. Place in cold water and set aside until ready to use. In each pan, place 2 tablespoons melted butter, 1 tablespoon water, a drop of saffron water, a pinch of salt and pepper. Mix well with a rubber spatula until creamy. Place rounds of potatoes side by side in each pan and fill the pan with parboiled rice from step 2 on the facing page. Pour a tablespoon of melted butter, a tablespoon water and a drop of saffron water over the top of the rice. Cover the entire pan with a piece of oiled aluminum foil. **Press down** over the aluminum foil and seal tightly so that steam cannot escape. Bake for **45** minutes in the preheated 500°F oven.

Individual Lavash Bread Rice Crusts *Tah dig-e fardi-e nun*

For this recipe eliminate the yogurt base and use lavash bread for the crust. In each pan, place 2 tablespoons melted butter, 1 tablespoon water, a drop of saffron water, a pinch of salt and pepper. Mix well with a rubber spatula until creamy. Place a 6-inch-diameter disc of lavash bread in each pan before filling them with parboiled rice from step 2 on the facing page. Pour a tablespoon of melted butter, a tablespoon water and a drop of saffron water over the top of the rice. Cover the entire pan with a piece of oiled aluminum foil. **Press down** over the aluminum foil and seal tightly so that steam cannot escape. Bake for **40** minutes in the preheated 415°F oven.

Serving Note

Place an individual crust rice, crust up or crust down according to your fancy, in the center of a large, warm plate. Serve with a braise by first placing the meat over the rice, top with vegetables and spoon the juice evenly all over. Garnish with herbs or edible flowers.

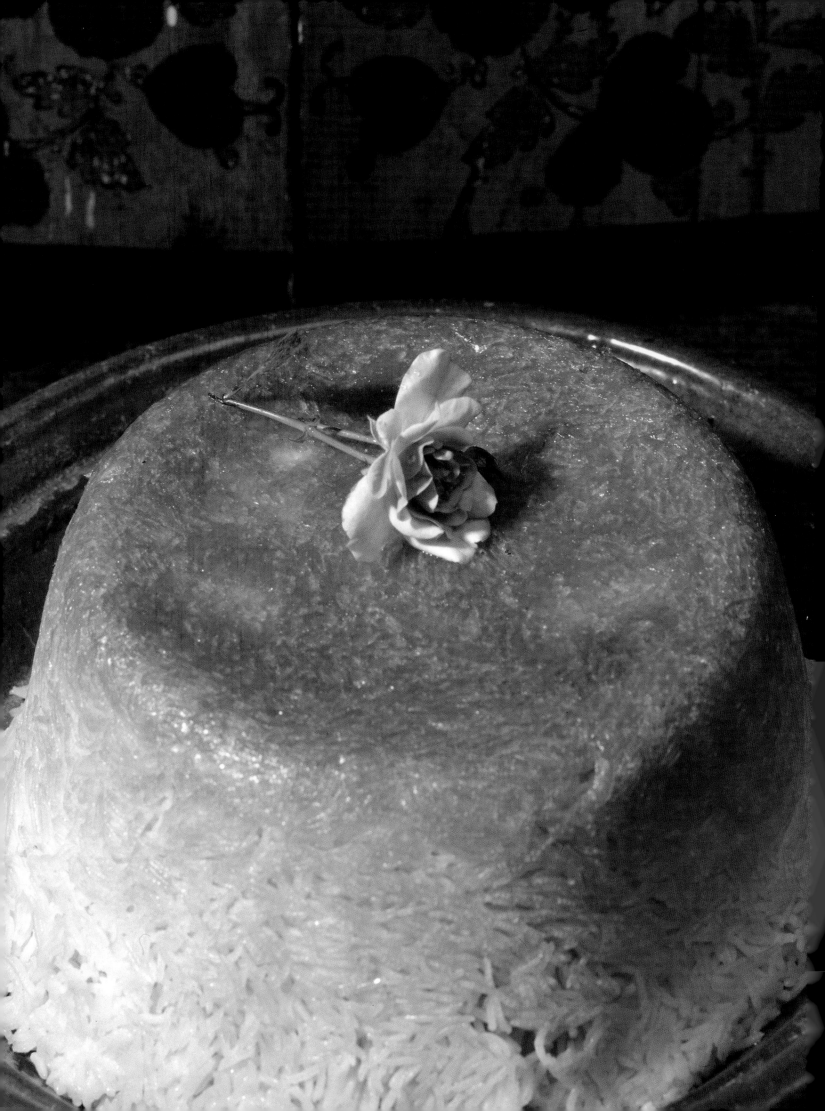

Saffron Steamed Plain Rice: Rice Cooker Method

Chelow ba polow paz

Servings: 6
Preparation time: 10 minutes
Cooking time: 1 hour 30 minutes

3 cups long-grain basmati rice (among long-grained types of rice, choose those that are long, thick and sleek at the tip)
5 cups water
1 tablespoon salt
1/4 cup oil
1/4 cup butter or ghee (clarified butter)
2 cardamom pods
2 bay leaves

Garnish
1/4 teaspoon ground saffron, dissolved in 1 tablespoon hot water

Note
If you use Texmati rice, use 3 cups water for 3 cups rice.
If using **brown** basmati rice, use 6 cups water for 3 cups rice.

This is a wonderfully fast and trouble-free way to make white rice for the home as well as for restaurants. Wash the rice; add water, salt and oil; push the button and in about 30 to 35 minutes you will have excellent rice. Of course, if you want to get the golden crust then allow 1 to 1 1/2 hours, depending on your type of rice cooker.

1. Clean and wash 3 cups of rice 5 times in warm water and drain.

2. Combine all the ingredients except the saffron water in the rice cooker; gently stir with a rubber spatula and start the rice cooker.

3. After 1 to 1 1/2 hours (cooking times may vary according to the type of rice cooker; for National Deluxe it is 1 1/2 hours, for Pars, it is 1 hour), open the lid and pour the saffron water over the rice. Cover and unplug the rice cooker.

4. Allow to cool for 10 minutes covered.

5. Remove lid and place a round serving dish over the pot. Hold the dish and the pot tightly together and turn them over to unmold the rice. The rice will be like a cake. Cut into wedges and serve.

Serving Note

This rice will go well with any of the main course meats or fish, and particularly well with Yogurt and Saffron-Infused Chicken Braise (see page 182) or the Roast Pheasant with Caramelized Quince Braise (see page 176).

Wine Note

All wines are welcome.

Spring-Lamb Shank Braise in Merlot, Saffron & Rosewater with Fava Bean & Dill Steamed Rice with Lavash Crust

Baqala polow ba mahicheh-ye barreh

Servings: 6
Preparation time: 20 minutes
Cooking time: 3 hours

6 lamb shanks
3 teaspoons salt
2 teaspoons freshly ground pepper
2/3 cup all-purpose flour
6 tablespoons oil
1 bulb garlic, peeled and sliced
4 onions, peeled and diced
2 tablespoons orange rind
Zest of 1 lime
1 cinnamon stick (4 inches)
1 teaspoon saffron, ground and
 dissolved in 1/4 cup rosewater
1 tablespoon honey
2 cups water
4 cups Merlot wine
1 tablespoon fresh lime juice
 (optional)

Garnish
8 onions thinly sliced and 1 red
 pepper shredded, and deep fried
 golden, drained over paper towel
2 cups drained yogurt

Pickled Radishes
Place a bunch of washed radishes
 in a colander and sprinkle with 1
 teaspoon salt. Rinse and transfer to
 a nonreactive bowl. Add 2 teaspoons
 grape molasses and 1/2 cup vinegar
 and leave for 30 minutes and up to
 24 hours.

Lamb Shanks

1. Preheat oven to 325°F.

2. Wash the shanks and pat dry. Dust with salt and pepper, and dredge in the flour. Set aside.

3. Heat 3 tablespoons oil in a large enough ovenproof baking dish to fit 6 lamb shanks and fry the shanks until golden brown on all sides. Add the onion, garlic, orange rind, lime zest and cinnamon, and cook for 10 minutes. Add saffron rosewater, honey, water and wine; bring to a boil. Remove from heat.

4. Cover and bake the shanks in the preheated oven for 2 1/2 to 3 hours, or until tender.

5. Remove the baking dish from the oven. Reduce oven to low.

6. Adjust seasoning to taste (add salt, pepper, honey, rosewater, lime juice as necessary). Cover and keep warm until ready to serve.

Fava Bean & Dill Steamed Rice recipe continued on the following pages.

Servings: 6
Preparation time: 20 minutes
Cooking time: 1 hour 15 minutes

2 pounds fresh fava beans (in the
  pod) or 1 pound frozen (shelled)
3 cups long-grain basmati rice
3 tablespoons salt
1/4 teaspoon turmeric
1 1/4 cups melted butter or olive oil
1 teaspoon ground saffron, dissolved
  in 1/4 cup hot water
6 cups fresh dill weed, finely chopped
4 cloves garlic, peeled and chopped,
  or 6 whole green garlic, trimmed and
  chopped
1 teaspoon ground cinnamon

Crust
6 discs (six inch diameter) of lavash
  bread cut to fit the bottom of the
  individual pans
1 cup and 2 tablesoons butter,
  melted

Special Utensils
6 nonstick pans (6 inches in diameter
  each) or large muffin pans

Note
Soak herbs in a large container,
change water several times and wash
thoroughly—in Persian food, where
herbs are used in large quantities,
this is particularly important,
especially when using organic herbs.

Variation
Pistachio Rice
Replace fava beans with 1 pound
raw, unsalted pistachios (shelled) and
1 cup currants.

Fava Bean & Dill Steamed Rice with Lavash Crust

1. Shell beans from pods and remove outer layer of skin. If using frozen fava beans, soak in warm water for a few minutes, then peel.

2. Pick over and wash 3 cups of rice 5 times in a large container of warm water. Drain.

3. Bring 10 cups of water and 3 tablespoons of salt to a boil in a large, nonstick pot. Pour the rice into the pot. When the water boils again, add the fava beans and turmeric to the pot while water is boiling (turmeric helps the greens stay green).

4. Boil briskly for 6 to 10 minutes, stirring gently a few times with a wooden spoon to loosen any stuck grains (when the rice rises to the surface, it is ready). Remove from heat and drain in a large mesh colander. Rinse with 3 cups cold water.

5. Add the dill gradually to the colander and toss to mix the rice, dill, garlic and cinnamon evenly.

6. Preheat oven to 415°F. In each nonstick, 6-inch pan, place a tablespoon butter, a tablespoon water and a drop of saffron water. Mix well with a rubber spatula until creamy.

7. Place 1 lavash bread disc in each pan.

8. Fill each pan with a mixture of the parboiled rice, beans and dill mixture. Place 2 tablespoons butter, a tablespoon water and a drop of saffron water on top of each pan of rice.

9. Cover each pan entirely with a piece of oiled aluminum foil, **press down** over the foil and seal tightly, so that steam cannot escape, and bake for 35 to 40 minutes (depending on your oven) in the preheated oven.

10. Remove the pans from the oven and place them on a damp surface for 1 minute to cool, without uncovering them.

11. To unmold the rice, loosen the edges with a rubber spatula and turn each pan, one at a time, quickly onto a baking sheet (tap slightly, if necessary, to unmold). Keep warm, **uncovered,** in the oven until ready to serve (this rice is at its crustiest-outside and fluffiest-inside best when served immediately).

Serving Note

Serve on large individual plates with a rice crust, a lamb shank with
2 tablespoons of sauce and a tablespoon of crispy deep-fried onions.
Garnish with shredded red pepper, a dollop of plain drained yogurt and 2
tablespoons pickled garlic (see page 204).

Wine Note

Powerful green, earthy flavors of fava, herbs and saffron mirror similar
flavors in a dry Riesling, but overall this is a red wine dish. Pinot Noir for
the saffron, Merlot for the dill and cinnamon, and Cabernet Sauvignon for
the favas, yogurt and, of course, the lamb!

Now that you're old, drink wine, a glass or two—
Drink, though your hands shake, as you used to do;
What games the heavens have played with you! Drink wine,
And laugh at everything they've done to you.

Khalili/Davis

چنین پیش شیری بالا چخذ این نم شتر پمایه مرید ست لرزان نم شتر

باز گرچرخ با تو بازیها کرد برازلراو مخنده و خند این نم شتر

Duck Braise in Merlot & Pomegranate on Wedding Rice

Javaher polow ba ordak

Servings: 6
Preparation time: 20 minutes
Cooking time: 1 hour 40 minutes

2 tablespoons oil
6 large duck legs, trimmed of extra
  fat, skin scored
1 teaspoon salt
1 teaspoon freshly ground pepper
2 tablespoons flour
2 large onions, peeled and thinly
  sliced
4 cloves garlic
3 cups toasted shelled walnuts (about
  3/4 pound)
4 cups pomegranate juice or 1/2 cup
  pomegranate paste (diluted in 4
  cups water)
2 cups peeled and chopped butternut
  squash, cut in 1-inch cubes (about
  1/2 pound)
1/3 cup honey or grape molasses
1/4 teaspoon ground saffron,
  dissolved in 1 tablespoon hot water
1 cinnamon stick (4 inches)
2 cups Merlot wine

Servings: 6
Preparation time: 30 minutes plus
  8 to 24 hours marination
Cooking time: 10 minutes

6 duck breasts (8 ounces each)

Marinade
6 tablespoons verjuice
3 tablespoons grape molasses

Garnish
1 cup fresh pomegranate arils (about
  3 pomegranates)
1/4 cup toasted shelled walnuts
Thyme sprigs (optional)

Duck Legs

1. Preheat the oven to 325°F.

2. Heat the oil in an ovenproof sauté pan or Dutch oven (large enough for 6 duck legs), over medium-high heat.

3. Dust the duck legs with salt, pepper and flour, place them in the pan skin sides down, and fry all sides until golden. Remove, set aside and cover to keep warm.

4. Heat 2 more tablespoons oil in the same pan and brown the onion and garlic; transfer to a food processor. Add the toasted walnuts and grind finely. Add 1/2 cup of pomegranate juice and pulse to create a smooth paste. Transfer to the pan.

5. Add the remaining pomegranate juice, butternut squash, honey, saffron water, cinnamon stick, wine and the duck legs to the pan. Bring to a boil and simmer, uncovered, for 10 minutes.

6. Cover and bake in the oven for 1 1/2 hours or until the duck is tender. Keep warm until ready to serve.

Grilled Duck Breast

1. To marinate the duck breast, mix together all the marinade ingredients. Trim the fat off the duck skin, score the skin and place in the marinade. Cover and allow to marinate in the refrigerator overnight.

2. Generously sprinkle salt and pepper on both sides of each breast.

3. Place the duck breast skin side down on a hot grill (or under the broiler) for 6 minutes or until brown.

4. Turn over and grill the other side for about 2 to 3 minutes. Remove from the grill, cover and allow to rest for a few minutes. Cut each breast lengthwise into 6 diagonal slices.

Wedding Rice recipe continued on the following pages.

Serving Note

Combine a duck leg and slices of duck breast on a large, warm plate. Place one of the rice crusts on the side and spoon some sauce over the duck. Garnish just prior to serving by sprinkling with fresh pomegranate arils (when in season), toasted walnuts and sprigs of thyme.

Wedding Rice

1. Clean and wash 3 cups of rice 5 times in warm water and drain.

2. Melt 2 tablespoons butter in a skillet over medium heat, add the barberries and sauté for 20 seconds (be careful—barberries burn easily). Remove the barberries from the skillet and set aside.

3. In the same skillet melt 2 tablespoons butter and add the orange rind, carrot, 1 cup sugar, orange blossom water, cardamom and cinnamon. Stir fry for 2 minutes. Add 1 cup water and bring to a boil; reduce heat and simmer for 10 minutes. Drain, reserving the syrup. Add the pistachios and almonds and set aside.

4. Bring 8 cups water and 2 tablespoons salt to a boil in a large, nonstick pot. Pour the washed and drained rice into the pot. Boil briskly for 6 to 10 minutes, gently stirring twice to loosen any grains that may have stuck to the bottom. When the rice rises to the surface, it is ready to be drained.

5. Drain the rice in a large, fine-mesh colander and rinse with 3 cups cold water. Gradually add the orange and carrot mixture to the colander and toss to mix with the rice evenly.

6. Preheat oven to 415°F.

7. To make individual rice crusts, in each 6-inch nonstick pan place 1 tablespoon melted butter, a tablespoon water and a drop of saffron water, and mix with a rubber spatula until creamy. Place a disc of the lavash bread in each pan.

8. Fill each pan with the rice, orange and carrot mixture, and a tablespoon of barberries. Pour 1 tablespoon of the reserved syrup, 1 tablespoon of melted butter and a tablespoon of water over the rice in each pan.

9. Cover with oiled aluminum foil, press down on top of the aluminum and seal tightly around the rim so steam cannot escape. Bake in the preheated oven for 35 to 40 minutes. Remove from the oven, do not uncover, and place on a damp surface on the counter for 1 minute to cool.

10. To unmold the rice, remove the aluminum foil, loosen the edges with a rubber spatula, turn each pan, one at a time, quickly onto a baking sheet (tap slightly, if necessary, to unmold). Keep warm, **uncovered,** in the oven until ready to serve (this rice is at its crustiest-outside and fluffiest-inside best when served immediately).

Wine Note

In this dish the line between sweet and savory is a little vague. The spice and pomegranate amplify the duck's rich meat, with the grape essence adding sweetness; yet just when it seems too much, the acidity of citrus and verjuice bring it all back into harmony. Bigger wines like Chardonnay, Merlot and Cabernet Sauvignon are most effective here. Their alcohol and oak flavors are tamed by the dish, while the complex flavors need a wine as rich as they are.

Servings: 6
Preparation time: 40 minutes
Cooking time: 1 hour 15 minutes

3 cups long-grain basmati rice
1 cup and 2 tablespoons butter, melted
1 cup barberries, picked over, washed thoroughly and drained
1 cup slivered orange rind
2 large carrots (about 1/2 pound), peeled and cut into thin strips
1 cup sugar or grape molasses
1 tablespoon orange blossom water
1 teaspoon ground cardamom
1/2 teaspoon ground cinnamon
1 cup water
1/2 cup pistachios, unsalted
1/2 cup blanched sliced almonds, toasted
2 tablespoons salt
1/2 teaspoon ground saffron threads, dissolved in 2 tablespoons hot water
6 discs (6 inches in diameter each) of lavash bread cut to fit the bottom of the individual pans

Special Utensils
6 nonstick pans (6 inches in diameter each) or large nonstick muffin pans

Steamed Bulgur with Mung Beans & Dill

Dami-e balghur-o mash

Servings: 4
Preparation time: 20 minutes
Cooking time: 50 minutes

1 cup mung beans, picked over and washed
4 1/2 cups broth (fish, chicken or beef)
1 tablespoon salt
1/4 cup vegetable oil
2 tablespoons butter
2 tablespoons cumin seeds
2 large onions, peeled and thinly sliced
1 inch fresh ginger, peeled and grated
2 cloves garlic, crushed and peeled
2 Thai bird or serrano chilies, seeded and chopped
2 cups coarse bulgur
1/2 teaspoon freshly ground black pepper
1/2 teaspoon ground turmeric or saffron
1 large fresh tomato, peeled and sliced

Garnish
2 cups chopped fresh dill, or parsley, cilantro or basil
1 tablespoon butter

Variation
For steamed bulgur with lentils, replace the mung beans with brown lentils and 1 cup currants.

Bulgur was very popular in medieval Persian cooking, but it was gradually replaced with rice. Bulgur is created by removing the husk of the wheat and steaming, drying and crushing the berries. Do not confuse bulgur with cracked wheat. Bulgur is presteamed and needs very little cooking, whereas cracked wheat must be cooked in broth or water.

1. Combine the mung beans, 4 1/2 cups broth and 1/2 teaspoon salt in a medium-sized saucepan and bring to a boil. Reduce heat, partially cover and cook over medium heat for 20 minutes, until beans are almost tender. Set aside without draining the broth.

2. Meanwhile, heat the oil and butter in a medium-sized pot until very hot. Add the cumin and cook for 10 seconds, until aromatic (keep a cover handy to stop any seeds from flying out). Add the onion and fry for 10 to 15 minutes until golden brown. Add the ginger, garlic, chili and bulgur, and stir-fry for 2 minutes, until the bulgur browns lightly. Add 2 teaspoons salt, pepper, turmeric, tomato and mung beans (including the broth). Stir gently once and bring to a boil.

3. Reduce heat to medium-low, cover and cook for 20 minutes, or until all the liquid has been absorbed. Keep warm until ready to serve.

Serving Note

Just before serving add the dill and butter, and fluff gently with a fork. Serve on the side of lamb shanks (see page 162), or with chicken or fish.

Wine Note

Bulgur has a distinct meaty flavor—the addition of spice, fresh herbs and chilies add complexity. Go for a Zinfandel or a Shiraz; these will pair nicely with both the bulgur and sweet/hot spice notes.

Pan-Roasted Quail Infused with Verjuice Served with Tart Cherry Rice & Lamb Meatballs under a Lavash Bread Crust

Albalu polow ba kufteh-o belderchin

Servings: 6
Preparation time: 20 minutes plus
 8 to 24 hours marination
Cooking time: 10 minutes

12 semi-boned quails (leg and wing
 intact) or 3 Cornish hens, halved
2 tablespoons butter
1 tablespoon canola oil

Marinade
6 cloves garlic, peeled and crushed
1 inch fresh ginger, peeled and grated
1 cup olive oil
1 teaspoon ground saffron dissolved in
 2 tablespoons rosewater
1/2 cup grape molasses
 (shireh-ye angur)
1/3 cup verjuice (unfermented juice of
 unripe grapes)
2 tablespoons lime juice
3 teaspoons salt
2 teaspoons freshly ground black
 pepper

Glaze
1 tablespoon butter
1 cup tart cherry syrup

Quails

1. For the marinade, combine the garlic, ginger, olive oil, saffron rosewater, grape molasses, verjuice, lime juice, salt and pepper. Rub the inside and outside of the bird thoroughly with the marinade mixture.

2. Make an incision through the thigh of one leg of each quail and slide the end of the other leg through it to keep the legs together.

3. Place the quails in a nonreactive pan with the marinade, cover and marinate in the refrigerator for 8 hours and up to 24 hours.

Pan Roasting

1. In a baking pan, heat 2 tablespoons butter and 1 tablespoon oil and brown all sides of the quails. Remove from heat, cover and set aside.

2. Just before serving preheat oven to 500°F, uncover the quail and bake for 3 to 5 minutes, until done (up to 25 minutes for Cornish hens).

3. Meanwhile, make the glaze in a small saucepan by combining the butter with 1 cup tart cherry syrup and cook until you have a thick sauce.

4. Pour the tart cherry glaze over the baked quails.

Grilling

1. Turn on the grill until very hot.

2. Remove the birds from the marinade and skewer on metal skewers.

3. Grill each side 3 to 10 minutes or until golden and crisp.

4. Glaze the quail with the butter and tart cherry syrup mixture.

Tart Cherry Rice with Lamb Meatballs recipe continued on the following pages.

Servings: 6
Preparation time: 35 minutes
Cooking time: 1 hour 15 minutes

4 pounds fresh or frozen pitted tart
  cherries, or cherries in light syrup (3
  8 ounce jars), drained
2 cups sugar
1/2 cup grape molasses
1 cup butter
1/2 teaspoon cinnamon
1 tablespoon vegetable oil
1 large onion peeled and thinly sliced
1/2 teaspoon salt
1 pound ground lamb or beef
1 large onion, peeled and grated
1/2 teaspoon pepper
1/2 teaspoon turmeric
1/2 teaspoon ground cinnamon
1/2 cup vegetable oil
1 teaspoon ground saffron dissolved
  in 2 tablespoons rosewater
3 cups long-grain basmati rice
6 discs of lavash bread cut to fit the
  bottom of the individual pans

Garnish
1 tablespoon slivered almonds
2 tablespoons slivered pistachios
2 tablespoons melted butter
1/4 cup cherry syrup

Special Utensils
6 nonstick pans (6 inches in diameter
  each) or large nonstick muffin pans

Individual Tart Cherry Rice and Lamb Meatballs under a Lavash Bread Crust

1. Place cherries, sugar, grape molasses, 2 tablespoons butter and 1/2 teaspoon cinnamon in a medium-sized saucepan. Cook for 35 minutes over high heat. Remove from heat. Strain the cherries over a bowl until no syrup remains. Set cherries aside and save the syrup.

2. Heat 2 tablespoons oil in a wide nonstick skillet over medium heat and fry 1 onion until golden brown. Remove the onion with a slotted spoon and set aside.

3. To make the meatballs, combine ground meat, grated onion, 1/2 teaspoon salt, 1/2 teaspoon pepper, 1/2 teaspoon turmeric and 1/2 teaspoon cinnamon in a large mixing bowl. Knead with your hands and shape into bite-sized meatballs. Using the same skillet, heat 2 tablespoons butter over medium heat. Brown all sides of the meatballs by shaking the skillet back and forth. Pour 1/4 cup tart cherry syrup (from the syrup saved in step 1) and a drop of saffron water over the meatballs, and shake the skillet. Cover and keep warm.

4. Clean and wash the rice 5 times in warm water and drain.

5. Bring 8 cups water and 2 tablespoons salt to a boil in a large, nonstick pot. Pour the rice into the pot. Boil briskly for 6 to 8 minutes, gently stirring twice with a wooden spoon to loosen grains stuck together. When the rice rises to the surface, it is ready to be drained. Drain in a large, fine-mesh colander and rinse with 3 cups cold water.

6. Gradually add the cherries, meatballs and fried onions to the large, fine-mesh colander, and toss to mix evenly.

7. Preheat oven to 415°F. Place 1 tablespoon oil, 1 tablespoon water and a drop of saffron water into each 6-inch pan. Mix with a rubber spatula until creamy.

8. Place a disc of lavash bread in each pan. Cover with rice and tart cherries. Place a drop of saffron water, 2 tablespoons of butter and a tablespoon of tart cherry syrup over the rice mixture in each pan. Cover with oiled aluminum foil, **press down** on top of the aluminum and seal tightly around the rim, so steam cannot escape. Bake for 35 to 40 minutes.

9. Remove from the oven, place on a cool damp surface, do not uncover, and allow to rest for 1 minute. To unmold the rice, remove the aluminum foil, loosen the edges with a rubber spatula, turn each pan, one at a time, quickly onto a baking sheet (tap slightly if necessary to unmold). Keep warm, **uncovered** in the oven until ready to serve.

Serving Note

On large individual plates, place a rice crust, two quails, a few tart cherries, a spoon of syrup, a sprig of fresh herbs and meatballs

Wine Note

Tart cherry, almond, quail and ginger combine in an earthy, almost sweet way yet maintain enough savory character to keep it an entrée. It could be paired with a glass of late-harvest wine, but try it instead with Viognier or Zinfandel to bring out the quail's gamey, spicy character.

Khayyam, if wine's unmanned you, never fear, enjoy!
And if you're sitting with your lover here, enjoy!
Think how the world, and you, will end in nothingness:
Now that you're here, before you disappear, enjoy!

Khayyam/Davis

خیام اگر ز باده مستی خوش باش
درگه با صنمی و نشستی خوش باش
پایان همه چیر جهان نیستی است
پندار که نیستی چو هستی خوش باش

Chicken, Apricot & Rice in Pastry

Polow dar nan-e lavash

Servings: 6
Preparation time: 20 minutes
Cooking time: 1 hour 25 minutes

Filling

1/2 cup butter or ghee, or vegetable oil
1 cinnamon stick (4 inches)
2 tablespoons cumin seeds
1 teaspoon coriander seeds
5 green cardamom pods, bruised
2 pounds chicken thighs, boned and cut into bite-sized pieces
2 large onions, thinly sliced
2/3 cup blanched almonds
1/4 cup pistachios
2 large carrots (1/2 pound), peeled and thinly sliced
2 cups dried apricots, chopped
1 1/2 cups white basmati rice
3 cups chicken broth
2 teaspoons salt
2 tablespoons honey
1/2 teaspoon freshly ground pepper
1 cup currants
1 cup milk
1 tablespoon rosewater

Pastry

10-inch spring form cake pan (below)
1 cup butter or ghee, melted
1 package frozen filo pastry sheets (take the package out of the freezer and leave at room temperature for 2 hours); cover the filo while working to prevent it from drying
1 egg yolk, for the glaze

1. Heat 4 tablespoons butter in a wok or deep skillet over medium heat. Add the cumin, cinnamon, coriander and cardamom pods, and cook for 10 seconds, until they become aromatic (keep a cover handy to stop any seeds from flying out). Add the chicken and onions, and stir-fry for 10 minutes, until golden. Add the almonds, pistachios, carrots, apricots and rice, and stir-fry for 1 minute longer.

2. Add the broth and salt and bring to a boil. Reduce heat to medium, cover and cook for 15 minutes. Add the honey, salt, pepper, currants, milk and rosewater, cover and cook for 15 minutes longer. Remove from heat and allow to cool.

3. Preheat oven to 400°F.

4. Brush a 10-inch-diameter baking pan with some melted butter.

5. Lay the first sheet of filo pastry in the baking pan (allow the ends to hang well over the edges) and brush it with melted butter. Repeat this for 10 more sheets of filo, laying one over the other.

6. Place the filling in the center of the baking pan on top of the layers of filo. Fold the filo layers across and over the top of the filling. Place a sheet of filo over the top and tuck in any overlapping edges. Use your hands to form a round, smooth surface and brush the top of the pastry with the butter and egg yolk.

7. Bake in the center of the preheated oven for 40 minutes, or until the crust is crisp and golden.

Serving Note

Remove from oven, unclip the side of the pan and transfer to a round platter larger than the pastry. Cut into wedges and serve hot with a green salad.

Wine Note

Truly a magnificent dish that once again takes spicy, savory and sweet flavors and balances them all perfectly. The crust adds a rich buttery flavor that pairs nicely with oak-aged whites or reds. Go for a Chardonnay or dry Gewurztraminer in white; Pinot Noir or Cabernet if in the mood for red.

Roast Pheasant with Caramelized Quince Braise

Polow khoresh-e beh ba qarqavol

Servings: 4
Preparation time: 20 minutes
  plus 8 hours marination
Cooking time: 2 hours 30 minutes

2 pheasants (about 3 pounds each),
  fresh or defrosted
1/4 cup olive oil

Brine Marinade
8 cups water
1/2 cup coarse salt
1 large onion, peeled
4 cloves garlic, peeled
1 cup honey
1/4 cup grape molasses
3/4 cup verjuice
1 cinnamon stick (4 inches)
1/2 teaspoon ground saffron
1 tablespoon cumin seeds
5 kaffir lime leaves

Quince Braise
Preparation time: 20 minutes
Cooking time: 30 minutes

2 large quinces
3 tablespoons oil
2 tablespoons butter
2 large onions, peeled and thinly
  sliced
1 teaspoon salt
1/4 teaspoon freshly ground black
  pepper
1/4 teaspoon ground cinnamon
1/2 cup sugar
2 tablespoons grape molasses
1/4 cup fresh lime juice
1/4 cup wine vinegar
1/2 teaspoon ground saffron,
  dissolved in 2 tablespoons hot water
2 cups broth or water

Variation
This dish can also be made using two
chickens, or four Cornish hens, or 8
quails (baking times will vary).

1. Mix all the ingredients for the brine marinade in a large nonreactive pot. Bring to a boil, remove from heat and allow to cool.

2. Meanwhile clean the birds, rinsing inside and outside. Place the birds in the cool brine, cover and allow to marinate in the refrigerator for 8 to 24 hours.

3. Preheat oven to 350°F.

4. Generously oil a baking dish large enough for 2 pheasants.

5. Remove pheasants from marinade and drain. Place in the baking dish and brush the pheasants with olive oil all over.

6. Cover the baking dish with oiled aluminum foil and bake for 2 hours.

7. Uncover, baste the pheasants and bake uncovered for 15 to 30 minutes, until golden brown.

Quince Braise

1. Wash but do not peel the quinces. Cut into quarters, remove seeds, remove all hard parts of the inside of the quince and cut into 1-inch cubes.

2. Heat 3 tablespoons oil in a saucepan over medium heat, add the quince cubes and brown by shaking the pan. Remove quince cubes from the pan and set aside. Add 2 tablespoons butter. Add the onions and cook until golden brown. Add salt, pepper, cinnamon, sugar, grape molasses, lime juice, vinegar and saffron; cook over medium heat for 2 minutes, stirring well. Return the quince, stir and cook for about 5 minutes until the quince cubes are caramelized. Add the broth and bring to a boil. Reduce heat to medium-low, cover and cook for 20 minutes.

3. Taste the braise—it should be sweet and sour—and adjust the seasoning, adding lime juice or sugar as necessary. Cover and keep warm until ready to serve.

Serving Note

Place an individual portion of saffron steamed rice and pheasant in the center of a serving plate. Spoon some quince braise over the whole.

Wine Note

Savory and delectable, a seasonal way to serve pheasant that tames yet brings out its wild gamey flavor. A Riesling will cut the richness of the bird and bring out its sweetness. Pinot Noir will do the same if you prefer a red wine.

Saffron Chicken, Eggplant & Barberry Rice Cake

Shirazi polo-ye qalebi

Servings: 6 to 8
Preparation time: 30 minutes
Cooking time: 2 hours 30 minutes

3 cups white basmati rice
2 pounds chicken legs, boned,
  skinned and cut into 4-inch pieces
1 small onion, peeled and chopped
2 large onions, peeled and thinly
  sliced
1 teaspoon salt
1/2 teaspoon freshly ground black
  pepper
2 tablespoons fresh lime juice
1 teaspoon ground saffron dissolved
  in 1/4 cup rosewater
5 Chinese eggplants
1/2 cup vegetable oil
1 cup dried barberries *(zereshk)*,
1 cup butter or ghee
3 tablespoons honey, or sugar or
  grape molasses
2 cups plain yogurt
3 egg yolks
2 tablespoons chopped candied
  orange peel
1 tablespoon toasted cumin seeds

*This rice can be prepared, covered
and stored in the refrigerator for
up to 24 hours prior to cooking, but
make sure it is at room temperature before placing in the oven.*

1. Pick over the rice and wash the rice 5 times in warm water; drain and set aside.

2. Place the chicken and chopped onion in a medium-sized saucepan. Add salt, pepper, 1 tablespoon saffron and rosewater mixture, and fresh lime juice. Do not add water. Cover and simmer for 30 minutes over low heat.

3. Peel and cut eggplants lengthwise in 1/2-inch-thick slices. Rinse and blot dry.

4. Brush the eggplant slices with oil and place on a baking sheet. Grill under a hot broiler for 5 to 7 minutes, or until golden brown, on each side. Drain on a paper towel and set aside.

5. Heat 1/4 cup oil in a wide skillet over medium heat, add the sliced onion and cook until golden brown. Use a slotted spoon to remove from the skillet and set aside.

6. Barberries often have sand in them. Clean by soaking in a bowl of cold water for 10 minutes. Drain, rinse and set aside.

7. In the same skillet, add the barberries and 3 tablespoons honey, and stir-fry for 20 seconds. **Do not overcook the barberries. Be careful; they burn very easily.** Remove from heat.

8. Bring 8 cups water and 2 tablespoons salt to a boil in a large, nonstick pot. Pour the rice into the pot. Boil briskly for 6 to 10 minutes, or until the rice rises to the top, gently stirring twice to loosen any grains that may have stuck to the bottom. Drain rice in a large, fine-mesh colander and rinse with 3 cups cold water.

9. Preheat oven to 375°F.

10. Place about 1/2 a cup melted butter in a deep, ovenproof Pyrex dish (about 12 inches in diameter and 5 inches deep). Spread the butter evenly over the base and sides of the dish.

11. In a large mixing bowl, whisk the egg yolk and yogurt together until creamy. Add 2 spatulas full of rice, the candied orange peel, 1 tablespoon saffron water and the juice from the chicken, and mix well. Place this rice mixture in the ovenproof dish. Spread the rice mixture over the bottom, pressing it down with a rubber spatula, or use your hands.

12. Cover with 2 more spatulas of rice, then place the barberries, a layer of chicken, eggplant and onion on top of the rice and barberries. Add the remaining rice and sprinkle the cumin over the top. Pack it down into the dish using a rubber spatula. Pour remaining butter and saffron water over the top of the rice.

13. Cover with oiled aluminum foil, **press down** on top of the aluminum with your hands (this will help later in unmolding) and seal tightly around the rim so steam cannot escape. Bake in the oven for 1 1/2 to 2 hours, or until the crust is golden brown.

Serving Note

Remove the dish from the oven. **Do not uncover;** allow to cool on a damp surface for 15 minutes. Uncover and loosen the rice around the edges of the dish with the point of a knife. Place a large serving platter (larger than the rice mold) on top of the dish. Hold the dish and platter firmly together and turn over with a jolt to unmold the rice. Garnish with a few eggplant slices and a spoon of barberries over the top of the rice (I've used grapes for garnish in this photo). Serve hot.

Wine Note

This rich dish is full of flavor with acid and spice elements and a touch of sweetness. Because the elements are so well balanced, both white and red will work well. The chicken, crusted rice and saffron all are Chardonnay friendly, while the barberries, citrus and cumin call out for Merlot.

Lamb Meatballs & Unripe Grape Braise

Khoresh-e ghureh

Servings: 6
Preparation time: 30 minutes
Cooking time: 1 hour 25 minutes

1 pound ground lamb, turkey or fish
  fillets (boned and skinned)
2 onions, peeled: 1 medium, grated;
  1 large, thinly sliced
4 cloves garlic, peeled and crushed
2 teaspoons salt
1 teaspoon freshly ground black
  pepper
1/2 teaspoon turmeric
1/2 teaspoon ground cinnamon
1/4 teaspoon cayenne
1 cup and 2 tablespoons chopped
  fresh parsley
1/2 cup oil
5 stalks celery, washed and chopped
  into 1-inch lengths (4 cups,
  chopped)
1 cup fresh chopped cilantro
1 cup chopped fresh mint, or 2
  tablespoons dried
2 cups chicken broth or water
1/2 teaspoon ground saffron,
  dissolved in 2 tablespoons hot water
1 cup unripe grapes: for fresh,
  remove stems; in brine, drain
1 teaspoon honey

1. In a mixing bowl combine meat, 1 grated onion, 1 teaspoon salt, 1/2 teaspoon pepper, 1/2 teaspoon turmeric, 1/2 teaspoon cinnamon, 1/4 teaspoon cayenne, and 2 tablespoons parsley. Knead well. Shape into hazelnut-sized meatballs.

2. Heat 2 tablespoons oil in a large, nonstick skillet. Gently add the meatballs and cook over medium heat until golden brown. Shake the skillet back and forth to brown meatballs all over. Remove the meatballs with a slotted spoon and set aside.

3. Add 2 more tablespoons of oil to the same skillet and add the sliced onion and stir-fry for 10 minutes or until golden brown. Remove from the heat and set aside.

4. In a medium-sized heavy-bottom pot, heat 2 tablespoons oil over medium high. Add the celery and the remaining salt and pepper, and stir-fry for 10 minutes or until the celery is translucent. Add the herbs and stir-fry for 10 minutes longer.

5. Add the meatballs and the onions to the pot. Pour in the broth and bring to a boil. Reduce heat to low, cover and simmer for 30 minutes.

6. Add saffron water, the unripe grapes and honey. Stir once. Cover and cook over medium heat for another 15 to 20 minutes or until the celery is tender.

7. Taste the braise and adjust seasoning to taste. Cover and keep warm until ready to serve.

Serving Note

Place some saffron steamed white rice in the center of a warm plate, arrange the meatballs around it and spoon the braise with the unripe grapes over them.

Wine Note

Combine rich lamb, tangy green grapes, spice and honey in one dish and the result is perfect for Pinot Noir. Pinot acidity matches that of the green grapes and the spice in the braise is matched by the wine.

Yogurt & Saffron-Infused Chicken Braise

Khoresh-e mast-o zaferan

Servings: 4
Preparation time: 15 minutes
Cooking time: 65 minutes

Garnish
2 tablespoons vegetable oil, butter or ghee
1/2 cup blanched almonds
1/2 cup raisins
1 green apple, peeled & sliced
2 cups fresh basil leaves

Braise
2 tablespoons vegetable oil, butter or ghee
2 pounds boneless chicken thigh cut up into bite-sized pieces
2 small onions, peeled and thinly sliced
1 cup chopped celery
2 cloves garlic, peeled and sliced
1 teaspoon coriander seeds
1 inch fresh ginger, peeled and grated
5 kaffir lime leaves
1/2 teaspoon red chili flakes
2 teaspoons salt
1/2 teaspoon freshly ground black pepper
1/2 teaspoon ground saffron threads, dissolved in 2 tablespoons hot water
3 tablepoons grape molasses
2 tablespoons fresh lime juice
1/2 teaspoon orange rind (rind from about half an orange)
2 cups plain yogurt mixed with 1 teaspoon corn starch

Variation 1
This braise can be turned into a curry braise by replacing the saffron water and orange rind with 2 teaspoons hot curry powder.

Variation 2
Replace yogurt with coconut milk and replace the chicken with 2 pounds fish fillets cut into bite size pieces.

1. In a deep skillet, heat 2 tablespoons oil over medium heat until very hot. Add the almonds, raisins and apple, and stir-fry for 20 seconds. Remove with a slotted spoon and set aside.

2. Heat the remaining oil in the same skillet until very hot. Add chicken and onions, and stir-fry for 5 minutes, until translucent. Add the celery, garlic, coriander and ginger, and stir-fry for 1 minute longer. Add lime leaves, chili, salt, pepper, saffron water, grape molasses, lime juice and orange rind. Cover and cook over very low heat for 30 minutes.

3. Meanwhile, in a mixing bowl, beat the yogurt mixture in one direction for 5 minutes and gradually add it to the skillet over very low heat, stirring gently and constantly to prevent curdling.

4. Adjust seasoning to taste and simmer over low heat for 25 minutes. Cover and keep warm until ready to serve.

Serving Note

Place a portion of rice in the center of a warm plate and spoon the saffron braise around it. Garnish with the almond, raisin and apple mixture, and fresh basil.

Wine Note

Persian cuisine often surprises with its subtlety and nuance. Saffron, citrus and apples are balanced with yogurt, giving the braise a creamy, aromatic delicacy. This harmony allows a wide variety of wines to pair well. Sauvignon Blanc, Riesling, Chardonnay, Pinot Noir, Grenache, Shiraz and Merlot—all are a success.

Chicken & Eggplant Braise with Unripe Grapes

Khoresh-e ghureh-o jujeh-o bademjan

Servings: 4
Preparation time: 40 minutes
Cooking time: 1 hour 35 minutes

3 tablespoons olive oil
1 1/2 pounds chicken legs with skin and all visible fat removed, rinsed, patted dry and dusted with a mixture of 1 teaspoon salt, 1 teaspoon pepper, 1/2 teaspoon turmeric and 1 tablespoon flour
2 medium onions, peeled and thinly sliced
2 cloves garlic, peeled and crushed
1 cinnamon stick (4 inches)
1 teaspoon ground saffron, dissolved in 1/4 cup hot water
2 large tomatoes, pureed (2 cups)
1 cup unripe grapes *(ghureh)*, fresh in season or jarred in brine, drained (available at specialty stores)
4 tablespoons fresh lime juice
9 Chinese eggplants

Garnish
1 cup virgin olive oil
2 large onions, peeled and thinly sliced
1 large tomato, peeled and quartered

1. Heat 2 tablespoons oil in an ovenproof sauté pan, brown the chicken, add the onion, garlic and cinnamon, and sauté over medium heat, stirring occasionally with a wooden spoon, for 20 minutes. Add the saffron water.

2. Pour in 2 cups tomato puree, unripe grapes and lime juice. Cover and simmer over low heat for 30 minutes.

3. Peel the eggplants and cut lengthwise in quarters. Rinse with cold water and blot dry. Brush each side of the eggplant with oil and place on a baking sheet. Grill the eggplant on both sides until golden brown, about 5 minutes on each side. Set aside.

4. For the garnish, heat the oil in a deep skillet or deep fryer and deep-fry the onion over medium heat until golden brown; remove, drain and set aside. In the same skillet, sauté the tomato for garnish, remove from the skillet and set aside.

5. Preheat the oven to 350°F. Arrange the eggplant, fried onion and sautéed tomato over the chicken; cover and bake for 30 minutes. Uncover and bake for another 15 minutes.

6. Adjust seasoning to taste, garnish and keep warm in the oven until ready to serve.

Serving Note

Spoon individual portions onto a warm plate and serve with rice or bread.

Wine Note

A braise with the best combination of flavors: chicken, saffron and unripe grapes—spice, fruit and acid. Smells like a Chardonnay! They do mirror each other beautifully but so does a Viognier. Even a Cabernet Sauvignon, though it contrasts more than mirrors, is a happy pairing.

Lamb Shank & Aromatic Herbs with Red Beans & Dried Lime Braise on Steamed Rice Crust

Khoresh-e qormeh sabzi ba chelow

Servings: 4
Preparation time: 25 minutes
Cooking time: 3 hours 20 minutes

1/2 cup oil or butter
4 lamb shanks (about 2 pounds)
2 large onions, peeled and thinly sliced
1/3 cup dried red kidney beans, rinse and soaked in cold water for 30 minutes, drained
4 whole dried Persian limes *(limu-omani),* pierced
4 cups finely chopped fresh parsley or 1 cup dried
1 cup finely chopped fresh chives (or 1/4 cup dried) or spring onions
1 cup finely chopped fresh coriander
1 cup chopped fresh fenugreek leaves, or 1/4 cup dried
4 tablespoons verjuice
1/2 teaspoon ground saffron, dissolved in 2 tablespoons hot water

Note
Soak herbs in a large container, change water several times and wash thoroughly—in Persian food, where herbs are used in large quantities, this is particularly important, especially when using organic herbs.

1. In an ovenproof sauté pan, heat 3 tablespoons oil and brown the shanks on all sides and remove from the pan. Add the onions and fry until golden brown. Add beans, whole dried Persian limes, lamb shanks and 4 cups of water. Bring to a boil, cover and simmer for about 30 minutes over low heat, stirring occasionally.

2. Preheat oven to 350°F.

3. Meanwhile, heat the remaining oil in a large skillet over medium heat. Add the chopped parsley, chives, coriander and fenugreek, and fry stirring constantly, for 20 minutes, or until the aroma of frying herbs rises (this stage is very important for the taste of the braise).

4. Add the herbs, verjuice and saffron to the sauté pan. Cover and bake for 2 1/2 hours.

5. Check to see if meat and beans are tender. Taste and adjust seasoning. Reduce oven to warm and cover until ready to serve.

Serving Note

Place one lamb shank on a warm serving plate, place an individual steamed rice with crust (see page 159) beside it and spoon the sauce with beans over it.

Wine Note

Meaty shanks combine with tangy lime, green herbs and savory red beans and rice. Green and acid are key flavors in this dish—white and red wine can work. Try a powerful aromatic white such as a dry Australian Riesling or a blended red from southern Italy or Greece.

Persian Gulf-Style Striped Bass & Shrimp Braise with Tamarind

Qaliyeh-ye mahi-o meygu

Servings: 4
Preparation time: 20 minutes
Cooking time: 30 minutes

4 striped bass pieces (6 ounces
  each) or halibut, with skin on
4 jumbo shrimp, cleaned, washed,
  drained and patted dry

Spice Rub
1 teaspoon ground coriander seeds
1 teaspoon ground cumin seeds
1/4 teaspoon ground cinnamon
1/2 teaspoon turmeric
1 teaspoon salt
1 teaspoon freshly ground pepper
1/2 teaspoon red pepper flakes
1 tablespoon all-purpose flour

Cilantro Sauce
1/2 cup oil, butter or ghee
8 cloves garlic, peeled and chopped
1 teaspoon ground coriander seeds
1/2 teaspoon red pepper flakes
1/2 teaspoon turmeric
2 teaspoons salt
1/2 teaspoon pepper
3 cups chopped fresh cilantro leaves
1 cup fresh fenugreek or 1
  tablespoon dried fenugreek flakes
1/2 cup chopped fresh scallions
1/4 cup chopped fresh flat-leaf
  parsley
2 tablespoons all-purpose flour
2 tablespoons commercial tamarind
  paste (1/2 cup if homemade)
2 tablespoons verjuice or lime juice
1 teaspoon grape molasses
2 cups fish stock or water

1. To season the fish and shrimp: Make 3 slits with a sharp knife across the skin of the fish fillets. Devein and butterfly the shrimps. Season by lightly dredging in the spice rub mixture. Place in a flat dish, cover and keep in the refrigerator for at least 15 minutes and up to 24 hours.

2. To make the cilantro sauce, heat the oil over medium heat in a deep skillet. Add the garlic and stir-fry until lightly golden brown. Add coriander, red pepper flakes, turmeric, salt and pepper, and stir-fry for 1 minute.

3. Add the chopped herbs and stir-fry for 5 minutes. Add the flour and stir-fry for 20 seconds. Add the tamarind, verjuice, grape molasses and fish stock, and bring to a boil. Reduce heat to low, cover and cook for 15 minutes. Taste the sauce and adjust seasoning (add more tamarind paste, red pepper or salt according to taste). Cover and keep warm.

4. To make the fish and shrimp, heat 2 tablespoons oil in a large, nonstick skillet over medium-high heat until **very hot.** Add the fish, skin side down, and cook for about 2 minutes or until golden brown and crispy. Turn the fish over and fry the other side until cooked through and crispy on both sides. Remove the fish and set aside. Add more oil to the pan and sauté both sides of the shrimp until done (the color will change; don't overcook).

5. Just before serving add the fish and shrimp gently to the sauce and allow to simmer over very low heat for 5 to 10 minutes.

Serving Note

Place an individual rice crust or mound a cup of white rice in the center of a warm plate, and top with a piece of fish and a shrimp. Spoon the sauce over the whole. Garnish with a sprig of herbs on top.

Wine Note

A delicate yet meaty white fish, striped bass is well suited to the cumin, cilantro and tamarind flavors of this braise. Lightly balanced between green and tangy notes with just a hint of bitter, it is a good pairing with a dry Riesling or Gewurztraminer for whites. Pair with Pinot Noir for a delicate flavor or Cabernet Sauvignon for weight and intensity.

Sautéd Striped Bass in Bitter Orange & Grape Sauce

Mahi ba narenj-o shireh-ye angur

Servings: 4
Preparation time: 10 minutes
Cooking time: 30 minutes

4 thick, firm-fleshed whitefish
  (striped bass, rockfish) fillets, about
  2 pounds total
2 teaspoons salt
1 teaspoon freshly ground black
  pepper
2 tablespoons flour
4 tablespoons butter
2 tablespoons olive oil
8 cloves garlic, peeled
2 cups bitter orange juice or a
  mixture of 1 cup fresh lime juice
  and 1 cup fresh orange juice
3 tablespoons grape molasses
1/2 teaspoon ground saffron,
  dissolved in 2 tablespoons hot
  water and a teaspoon of orange
  blossom water
1/2 inch fresh ginger, peeled and
  grated
1/2 teaspoon red pepper flakes

Garnish
1/4 cup barberries, washed and
  sautéd in 1 tablespoon butter
1/2 cup fresh basil leaves

1. Rinse fish in cold water. Pat dry with a paper towel and dust both sides with 1 teaspoon salt, 1/2 teaspoon pepper and flour.

2. Heat half the butter and oil in a skillet over medium heat until very hot. Sauté the fish on both sides until golden brown. Remove from the skillet and keep warm.

3. In the same skillet add the remaining butter and garlic, and stir-fry until golden brown. Add bitter orange juice, grape molasses, 1 teaspoon salt, 1/2 teaspoon pepper, saffron water, ginger and red pepper flakes. Bring to a boil. Reduce heat and simmer for 10 minutes, or until a sauce is created. Adjust seasoning by adding more grape molasses or bitter orange juice.

Serving Note

Place a portion of fish beside fava bean and dill rice or on the top of a fava bean and dill rice crust (see page 164) and spoon the bitter orange sauce over the top. Add some herb kuku on the side and garnish with barberries and fresh basil or other herbs.

Wine Note

Viognier pairs well with the acidic orange and saffron spice, or a lighter red such as a Tempranillo will add savory flavors to this vibrant fish dish.

Pan-Seared Catfish with Sumac

Mahi-o somagh

Servings: 4
Preparation time: 20 minutes
Cooking time: 10 minutes

4 thick, firm-fleshed catfish fillets
2 tablespoons olive oil
Juice of 1 lime
1 teaspoon salt
1/4 teaspoon freshly ground black
  pepper
1/4 teaspoon cayenne pepper
1/2 cup sumac powder
1 tablespoon butter
1 tablespoon olive oil
8 cloves garlic, peeled
2 tablespoons grape molasses

1. Wash the fish and pat dry with a paper towel. Paint both sides with olive oil and sprinkle both sides with lime juice, salt, pepper, cayenne and sumac powder to completely cover. Cover and keep chilled for 15 minutes and up to 24 hours.

2. Heat 1 tablespoon butter and 1 tablespoon oil in a wide skillet over medium-high heat until very hot. Add the garlic and brown on all sides; remove from the skillet. Add the fish and brown each side for 4 to 5 minutes, or until the fish is tender. Return the garlic to the skillet and pour the grape molasses over the fish. Keep warm until ready to serve.

Serving Note

Place the catfish fillets in the center of a warm plate and place some mung bean and dill bulgur (see page 169) on top. Garnish with fresh herbs.

Veal Fillet Kebab in Saffron & Roses

Kabab-e Shahnameh-ye Ferdowsi

Servings: 4
Preparation time: 20 minutes
  plus 2 to 8 hours marination
Cooking time: 10 minutes

2 pounds lean loin (veal, lamb
  or beef)

Marinade
2 tablespoons olive oil
1 teaspoon salt
1 teaspoon freshly ground black
  pepper
Juice of 1 onion, peeled, pureed and
  strained
2 tablespoons lime juice
1/2 teaspoon ground saffron,
  dissolved in 2 tablespoons rosewater
2 cups Shiraz wine

Basting
1/2 cup butter

Cooking and Garnish:
6 flat 3/8 inch-wide skewers
1 package (12 ounces) of lavash
  bread
Pickles
Basil
Scallions
Coarse salt
Rose petals

Note
The way the meat is cut and
skewered for fillet kebab is important:
Cut the veal fillet, against the grain,
into 3-inch strips. Cut each of these
strips, along the grain, into 3 or
4 thin strips. Skewer these strips
against the grain.

1. Remove the backbone from the veal loins, remove the fillets from the loins, and trim off all fat and gristle from the main muscle. Cut meat lengthwise into 3-by-4-by-1/4-inch pieces (see note).

2. In a nonreactive container combine olive oil, salt, pepper, onion juice, lime juice, saffron rosewater and wine. Mix well. Add the meat and turn over in the marinade. Cover the meat and marinate for at least **2 hours and up to 8 hours** in the refrigerator. Turn the meat in the marinade twice during this period.

3. Start a bed of charcoal at least 30 minutes before you want to cook and let it burn until the coals glow. Or, switch on the grill until very hot.

4. Meanwhile, thread each piece of meat onto the flat, sword-like metal skewer, leaving a few inches free on both ends. Using another skewer, pound the meat with the narrow edge of the skewer to tenderize it.

5. For basting, melt the butter in a small saucepan and keep warm.

6. When coals are ready (**the key to cooking any kebab is a very, very hot grill**), brush meat lightly with the baste. Place the skewered meat on the grill. Cook for 3 or 4 minutes on each side, turning the skewers frequently. The meat should be seared on the outside, pink and juicy on the inside.

7. Spread lavash bread on a serving platter. When the meat is cooked, place the skewers of meat on the bread and brush them with the baste. Sprinkle with salt and rose petals. Cover with lavash bread to keep the food warm.

Serving Note

Kebabs are delicate pieces of meat and are best eaten hot off the grill—they suffer if kept warm after they are ready. Make sure everything else is ready before serving the kebabs. Serve with chelow (saffron steamed rice) or lavash bread, *torshi* (grape and garlic pickles) and a dish of fresh herbs, especially spring onions and basil. Loosen the first piece of meat on the skewer; hold all the meat down with the bread and pull out the skewer.

Wine Note

Veal fillet is always tender but not always flavorful. But when it is marinated then quickly cooked over a hot grill, one discovers how good fillet can be. Succulent and full of flavor, this kebab is the way to go with Shiraz or Merlot. The meat soaks up any tannin in the wine and the wine brings out the sweet earthiness in the beef.

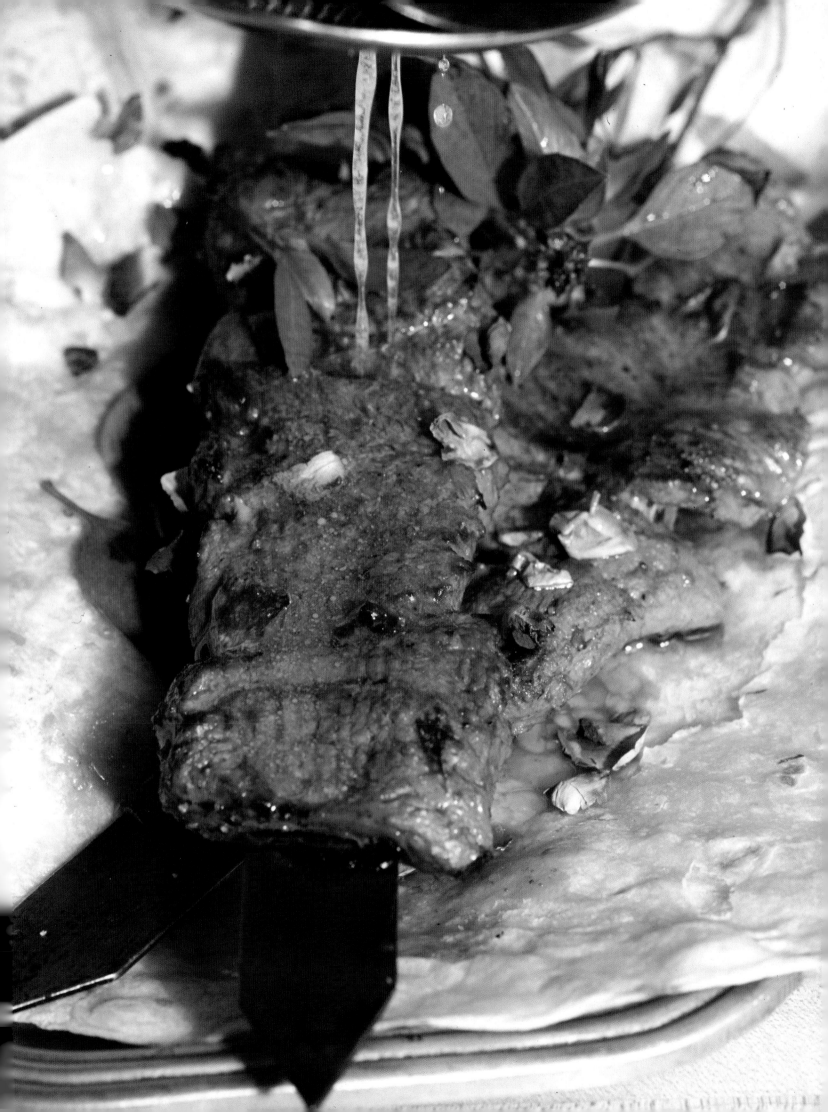

Lamb Kebab with Pomegranate Glaze

Chenjeh kabab ba anar

Servings: 4
Preparation time: 20 minutes
  plus 4 hours marination
Cooking time: 10 minutes

Marinade
2 pounds lean lamb tenderloin (ask
  butcher to remove backbones from
  the loins)
1 large onion, peeled, pureed and
  strained (keep the juice)
4 cloves garlic, mashed
1/2 cup fresh lime juice or verjuice
1 cup pomegranate juice
2 tablespoons olive oil
1 teaspoon salt
1 teaspoon freshly ground black
  pepper

Sweet & Sour Pomegranate Glaze
4 tablespoons grape molasses
4 tablespoons butter
2 tablespoons pomegranate paste
2 tablespoons Shiraz wine
1 teaspoon freshly ground black pepper
1 teaspoon salt
1/4 teaspoon red pepper flakes
2 teaspoons cornstarch diluted with 2
  tablespoons water

Also Needed
6 flat 1/8-inch-wide sword-like
  skewers
1 package (12 ounces) of lavash bread
1 cup pomegranate arils

Variation
This recipe can also be made using
2 pounds leg of lamb cut into 2-inch
cubes (marinate for at least 24 hours
and up to 3 days) or 16 lamb rib
chops (single cut).

Note
The way the meat is cut and
skewered for fillet kebab is important:
Cut the fillet, against the grain, into
3-inch strips. Cut each of these
strips, along the grain, into 3 or
4 thin strips. Skewer these strips
against the grain.

1. Fillet the loins and trim all the fat and gristle from the main muscles.

2. Cut meat into 3 by 4 by 1/4-inch strips.

3. Combine all the ingredients for the marinade in a nonreactive container and add the meat. Toss well. Cover and marinate for at least 4 hours and up to 2 days in the refrigerator.

4. In a saucepan, combine all the ingredients for the glaze until smooth. While whisking, bring the mixture to a boil. Remove from heat and set aside.

5. Start a bed of charcoal 30 minutes before you want to cook and let it burn until the coals glow, or turn on your grill until very hot.

6. In the meantime, thread 5 or 6 pieces of lamb onto each skewer, leaving at least 2 inches free on both ends of the skewers. **Make sure you skewer the meat against the grain.** Use another skewer or the blunt edge of a knife to gently pound kebabs against the grain. This will help tenderize them.

7. Once the coals are glowing, or the grill is very hot, cook one skewer of kebab in advance to check its flavor (cook's privilege). Cook for 1 or 2 minutes on each side, turning frequently. The meat should be seared on the outside, pink and juicy on the inside.

8. Baste with the spicy sweet and sour glaze.

Serving Note

Kebabs are delicate pieces of meat and are best eaten hot off the grill—they suffer if kept warm after they are ready. Make sure everything else is ready before serving the kebabs. Spread lavash bread on a serving platter. When the meat is cooked, place the skewers of meat on the bread. Sprinkle with pomegranate arils and coarse salt. Serve immediately with saffron steamed rice, and a dish of fresh herbs, which should include scallions and basil. Keep the meat on skewers until the last minute, because it will keep hot. Remove the meat from each skewer by placing a piece of lavash bread over several pieces of meat and using it to hold down the meat while you pull out the skewer.

Wine Note

The kebab is marinated in pomegranate for tangy acidity, with grape essence for sweetness, then grilled to caramelize it. Makes a great foil for wine. In the case of this lamb kebab you'll find it delicious with oaky Chardonnay, sexy with aromatic Pinot Noir; it struts with juicy Shiraz and canoodles with meaty Cabernet Sauvignon.

Chicken Kebab

Jujeh kabab

Servings: 4
Preparation time: 20 minutes
  plus 24 hours marination
Cooking time: 15 minutes

Marinade
1 teaspoon ground saffron, dissolved
  in 2 tablespoons hot water
1 cup fresh lime juice
1/4 cup olive oil
2 large onions, peeled and thinly sliced
2 cloves garlic, peeled and crushed
2 tablespoons zest of lime
2 tablespoons yogurt
2 teaspoons salt
2 teaspoons freshly ground black
  pepper

Kebab
4 Cornish hens, about 4 pounds,
  each cut into 10 pieces
5 medium tomatoes, halved

Baste
1/2 cup butter
Juice of 1 lime
1/2 teaspoon salt
1/2 teaspoon freshly ground black
  pepper

Cooking & Garnish
6 flat sword-like skewers
2 packages (12 ounces each) of
  lavash bread
2 limes, cut in half
Basil sprigs

Variation
Quail kebab can be cooked like
chicken kebab, but replace the
chicken marinade with the following
marinade for 8 partially boned quails:

8 cloves garlic peeled and mashed,
1 inch ginger root grated, 1/3 cup
grape molasses, 1 cup verjuice,
1 teaspoon freshly ground black
pepper, 1 teaspoon salt, 1/2
teaspoon ground saffron (dissolved in
2 tablespoons rosewater).

Marinate in the refrigerator for
1 to 3 days.

Make an incision through the thigh
of one leg of each quail and slide the
end of the other leg through it to keep
the legs together. Skewer the quails
whole, 3 to a skewer.

1. In a large, deep, nonreactive container with a cover, combine the saffron water, lime juice, olive oil, onions, garlic, lime zest, yogurt, salt and pepper. Beat well with a fork. Add the pieces of chicken and toss well in the marinade. Cover and marinate for at least 24 hours and up to 3 days in the refrigerator. Turn the chicken twice during this period.

2. Start a bed of charcoal 30 minutes before you want to cook and let it burn until the coals glow evenly. Otherwise, preheat the grill or oven broiler until very hot.

3. Skewer the tomatoes.

4. Spear wings, breasts, and legs onto different skewers (they require different cooking times).

5. For the baste, melt the butter in a small saucepan and add the juice of 1 lime. Add 1/2 teaspoon salt and 1/2 teaspoon pepper. Mix well and set aside.

6. Paint the tomato and chicken with the basting mixture. Cook a skewer of kebab in advance to adjust seasoning. Grill the chicken and tomatoes 8 to 15 minutes, until done. Turn frequently and baste occasionally. The chicken is done when the juice that runs out is yellow rather than pink.

Serving Note

Spread a whole lavash bread on a serving platter. Paint the chicken with the baste mixture. Remove the grilled chicken from skewers at the last minute and arrange the pieces on the bread. Garnish with lime juice and sprigs of basil. Cover the platter with more bread. Serve immediately with a bowl of fresh Persian or Thai basil leaves and scallions, and a Shirazi-style salad on the side.

Wine Note

The lime and onion marinade brings out the wild flavors in the bird so that when you pair it with Pinot Noir or Shiraz, the flavors just knock you out. Be warned though; once you try it, you'll be out grilling every day.

For quail kebab a Chardonnay will work best, adding a touch of sweetness to the quail. A Shiraz pairs well too, giving some nuance to the taste.

Ground Lamb Kebab & Yogurt Shallot Sauce

Kabab-e kubideh ba nun-o gojeh va mast-o musir

Servings: 6
Preparation time: 40 minutes
Cooking time: 10 minutes

Kebab
2 pounds lamb shoulder, twice ground
2 teaspoons salt
1 teaspoon freshly ground black pepper
1/2 teaspoon baking soda
1 tablespoon ground sumac
1 medium onion, peeled and finely grated

Cooking and Garnish
12 flat 1-inch skewers
1 package (12 ounces) of lavash bread
1/2 cup sumac powder
2 limes, cut in half
bowl of fresh basil leaves

Baste
2 tablespoons butter
1/2 teaspoon salt
1/2 teaspoon lime juice

Shallot Yogurt Salad
Mast-o musir

Servings: 4
Preparation time: 10 minutes plus overnight soaking and chilling
1/4 pound dried Persian shallots (*musir*) or 1 pound fresh
2 cups drained yogurt
1/2 teaspoon salt
1/4 teaspoon freshly ground black pepper

Note
If using fresh shallots, peel and chop shallots and soak in cold water overnight. Change the water several times. Drain and pat dry. If using dried shallots, place in a saucepan, cover with water, bring to a boil over high heat, reduce heat and simmer for 25 minutes or until tender. Drain, rinse with cold water and pat dry. Chop the shallots finely. In a mixing bowl combine the shallots with the yogurt, salt and pepper.

Variation
You can replace the lamb with ground boneless chicken thighs and 2 tablespoons olive oil.

1. In a warm mixing bowl, combine meat and the rest of the kebab ingredients. Knead with your hands for about 5 minutes to form a paste that will adhere well to the cooking skewers. Cover the paste and let stand for 15 minutes at room temperature.

2. Using damp hands, divide the meat paste into 12 equal lumps about the size of oranges. Roll each into a sausage shape 5 inches long and mold each one firmly around a flat, wide, sword-like skewer. Cover and keep in a cool place. Cook one skewer of the kebabs in advance under the broiler to adjust for seasoning.

3. Start a bed of charcoal at least 30 minutes before you want to cook and let it burn until the coals are glowing evenly.

4. For the baste, melt the butter in a small saucepan and add a pinch of salt and the lime juice.

5. Arrange the skewers on the **very hot** grill 3 inches above the coals (bricks make good platforms for grill use), keeping in mind that the ground meat should not touch the grill. **After a few seconds,** turn the meat gently to sear it, to help it attach to the skewers and to prevent it from falling off.

6. Grill the meat 3 to 5 minutes on each side, and brush with baste just before removing from the grill. Avoid overcooking. The meat should be seared on the outside, juicy and tender on the inside.

Serving Note

Kebabs are delicate and are best eaten hot off the grill—they suffer if kept warm after they are ready. Make sure everything else is ready before serving the kebabs. Spread lavash bread on individual serving plates. Loosen the meat from the skewers and slide it off using another piece of bread. Arrange the meat on the bread, sprinkle with sumac and lime juice to taste. Add a dollop of shallot yogurt salad (recipe on the left) and cover with more bread, which will help to keep it warm. Serve with fresh basil, grilled tomato, pickles, spring onions and Shirazi salad (see page 136). These kebabs can also be served with saffron steamed rice as well as or instead of the lavash bread.

Wine Note

A great ground meat kebab is moist, flavorful and slightly chewy. It also pairs well with wine; in fact this kebab pairs really well with rich white and red wines. Chardonnay, Shiraz and Cabernet Sauvignon love the flavors of the grill and so does *kubideh.*

Lamb Rib Chops

Shishlik-e Shandiz

Servings: 4
Preparation time: 20 minutes
  plus 2 days marination
Cooking time: 6 minutes

24 small, single lamb rib chops
  (French cut)

Marinade
1 large onion, thinly sliced
1 bulb garlic (10-12 cloves) peeled
  and crushed
2 tablespoons orange rind
1 cup fresh lime juice
2 teaspoons salt
2 teaspoons freshly ground black
  pepper
1/4 cup olive oil
1 cup plain yogurt
1/2 teaspoon ground saffron threads,
  dissolved in 2 tablespoon hot water
1 teaspoon grape molasses or honey

Basting
2 tablespoons melted butter
Juice of 2 limes
1/2 teaspoon coarse salt
1/2 teaspoon freshly ground black
  pepper

Cooking & Garnish
6 thin metal skewers or bamboo
  skewers soaked in water for 2 hours
1 package (12 ounces) lavash bread
1 bunch scallions
1 bunch rosemary

1. Rinse the lamb rib chops in a colander with cool water and pat dry thoroughly with paper towels.

2. Prepare the marinade by mixing all of its ingredients in a large, deep, nonreactive container. Rub the rib chops thoroughly on both sides, one at a time inside the dish, with marinade. Cover and marinate for 2 days (for best results) in the refrigerator. Turn the chops once during this time.

3. Start a bed of charcoal at least 30 minutes before you want to cook and let it burn until the coals glow, or turn on the oven grill or broiler until very hot.

4. Meanwhile, thread the chops flat side up onto flat skewers; the skewers will go through the bone, which is soft.

5. For basting, combine the butter, lime juice, salt and pepper in a small saucepan. Keep warm over very low heat.

6. When the coals are glowing, place the skewers on the grill. Grill for 2 to 3 minutes on each side, turning occasionally. The total cooking time should be 4 to 6 minutes. The chops should be seared on the outside and juicy on the inside. Baste the chops just before removing from the flame.

Serving Note

Kebabs are delicate and are best eaten hot off the grill—they suffer if kept warm after they are ready. Make sure everything else is ready before serving the kebabs. Spread lavash bread on a serving platter. When the chops are done baste both sides again. Then hold the skewers over the platter, steady the meat with some lavash bread and pull the skewers, leaving the chops on the platter. Sprinkle with a little coarse salt. Garnish with scallions and rosemary, and cover with lavash bread to keep warm. Serve immediately.

Wine Note

A high point of Persian cuisine is its wonderful and varied preparations of lamb. This lamb rib is redolent with saffron, onion and yogurt—brilliant with Shiraz. The tarry spice and meaty black fruit in the wine play off the tangy marinade and sweet, gamey meat from the grilled rib. The French Cote Roti or Hermitage are also excellent with these chops.

Sturgeon Kebab with Grape Molasses Dip

Kabab-e uzunbrun

Servings: 4
Preparation time: 20 minutes
  plus 8 hours marination
Cooking time: 10 minutes

2 pounds sturgeon (or swordfish or
  salmon), scaled, skin removed and
  boned
1 large onion, peeled and sliced
4 cloves garlic, peeled and crushed
1/4 cup fresh lime juice
1 cup tomato juice
1/4 cup olive oil
1 teaspoon salt
1/2 teaspoon freshly ground black
  pepper
1 teaspoon red pepper flakes

Baste
1/3 cup butter
1/2 teaspoon ground saffron,
  dissolved in 2 tablespoons hot water
1/2 teaspoon salt
1/2 teaspoon pepper

6 flat 3/8-inch-wide sword-like
  skewers
1 package (12 ounces) of lavash
  bread

Dip
1 cup grape molasses mixed with 1/4
  cup verjuice

I remember the very distinctive taste of sturgeon kebab, which would always be the first dish we had on arriving by the Caspian Sea for the holidays. Today, American sturgeon from Oregon is available at specialty fish markets and also through the Internet. If you cannot find sturgeon, you can use swordfish or salmon.

1. Wash the fish with cool water and pat dry with a paper towel. Cut into cubes and place in a mixing bowl.

2. Combine the onion, garlic, lime juice, tomato juice, olive oil, salt, pepper and red pepper. Pour over the fish, toss well, cover and place in the refrigerator to marinate overnight and up to 24 hours.

3. Start a bed of charcoal 30 minutes before you want to cook and let it burn until the coals are glowing evenly, or turn on the grill. Meanwhile, thread the cubes of fish onto the skewers.

4. To make the baste, in a saucepan, melt the butter, and add the saffron, salt and pepper.

5. Grill the fish for 3 to 4 minutes, turning frequently, brushing occasionally with the baste. Avoid overcooking; the fish should be seared on the outside, juicy and tender on the inside.

Serving Note

Serve two skewers of kebab over lavash bread with the dip on the side.

Wine Note

Take a gamey, meaty fish like sturgeon, marinate it, then grill to make a good match for a rich, oak-scented wine. Right? Definitely so with a ripe California Chardonnay; the big fruit is a natural with the oily fish. If you prefer red wine, Shiraz is the way to go—the oak, dark black fruit and spice tones in the wine are just right with this catch.

Unripe Grapes in Brine

Ghureh-ye shur

Makes: 2 pints
Preparation time: 40 minutes
Storage time: 10 days at least

2 pounds unripe grapes
2 tablespoons coarse salt for every 4
  cups of water
1/2 teaspoon sugar
1/2 cup vinegar

1. Wash the unripe grapes and remove the stems.

2. Fill a large pot with water and bring to a boil. Blanch the grapes, drain and set aside.

3. Sterilize canning jars in boiling water. Drain and dry thoroughly.

4. Fill the jar almost to the top with grapes.

5. Bring 2 tablespoons salt, 4 cups water, sugar and the vinegar to a boil and fill the jar to within 1/2 inch of the top with this hot liquid mixture; seal jars immediately.

6. Store for at least 10 days in a cool, dark place before using. Use these unripe grape pickles as a sour agent with fish or chicken, or in a braise.

Pickled Garlic

Torshi-e seer

Makes: 2 pints
Preparation time: 20 minutes
Storage time: 6 weeks before using

1 pound garlic bulbs
1/2 cup grapes syrup *(shireh-ye
  angur)*
1 quart vinegar or more
1 teaspoon coarse salt

1. Peel off just the first outside layer of the garlic bulbs.

2. Fill in the center of each bulb with 1 teaspoon grape molasses.

3. Sterilize canning jars in boiling water and dry thoroughly.

4. Fill the jars nearly to the top with garlic bulbs. Pour in vinegar to within 1/2 inch of the top. Add a pinch of salt to the top. Seal the jars.

5. Store in a cool, dark place for at least 6 weeks before using. Pickled garlic is at its best when 7 years old, when it becomes black and brown, and sweet, like a preserve.

Light & Dark Pickled Grapes

Torshi-e angur

Makes: 2 pints
**Preparation time: 20 minutes plus time
  to allow grapes to dry completely**
Storage time: 40 days before using

2 pounds black grapes (large, thick-
  skinned and seedless)
2 pounds white grapes (large, thick-
  skinned and seedless)
2 quarts (8 cups) wine vinegar
2 tablespoons coarse salt (1
  tablespoon coarse salt for every 4
  cups of vinegar)
1/2 cup grape molasses *(shireh-ye
  angur)*

1. Clip the grapes into small clusters. Fill a large container with cold water and add the grapes. Allow to rest for 5 minutes, then drain and spread on a clean sheet for several hours or until all the clusters are completely dry.

2. Sterilize canning jars in boiling water. Drain and dry thoroughly.

3. Pack the jar almost to the top with black and white grapes, arranging them in alternating layers. In a medium-sized laminated saucepan bring vinegar, salt and grape molasses to a boil over medium heat, reduce heat and simmer for 5 minutes. Remove from heat and allow to cool.

4. Fill the jar to within 1/2 inch of the top with the vinegar mixture; seal immediately. Store for at least 40 days in a cool, dark place before using.

The Persian winter solstice festival is on the longest night of the year, December 21 or 22, and is called shab-e yalda, which means birthday eve of the sun. The ceremony can be traced back to the primal concept of Light and Good against Darkness and Evil in ancient Iran. From this night, when evil is at its zenith, light begins to triumph as days grow longer and give more light. In the autumn, during the grape harvest, the people of the grape-growing regions of Iran, such as the Azerbaijan region, select some of the choicest black and white grapes in order to make pickles. This symbolic delicacy of light and dark grapes is then served at the winter festival's dinner, where family and friends stay up all night, keeping fires burning and lights glowing to help the sun in its battle against darkness. They recite poetry and play music, tell jokes and stories, talk and eat and eat and talk until the sun triumphantly reappears in the morning. It is believed that in this way they help good conquer evil.

The grape said to the farmer, "Sunlight fell
From far away and made my belly swell:
For a hundred days, and seventy, and three,
Here in the sun's bed, sunlight's served me well."

Manuchehri/Davis

به دهقان که پرسید از انگور

ملا خورشید کرد آبستنم از دور

حمیصر از صد و هفتاد و سه روز

بدم در بستر خورشید پرورد

DESSERTS, SHERBETS,
TEAS & BREWS

Raisin manufacturing near Qazvin, Iran.

Almond Baklava

Baqlava

Makes: 30 pieces
Cooking time: 35 minutes
Resting time: 2 hours

Syrup
2 1/2 cups sugar
1 1/2 cups water
1/2 cup rosewater
2 tablespoons lime juice

Filling
2 pounds blanched almonds, ground
2 cups sugar or grape molasses
2 tablespoons ground cardamom

Dough
1/4 cup plain milk
1/2 cup canola oil
1 tablespoon cooled syrup
1/4 cup cooking rosewater
1 large egg
2 1/2 cups unbleached all-purpose
   flour, sifted
4 tablespoons canola oil for baking

Garnish
2 tablespoons slivered pistachios
2 tablespoons dried rose petals

Variation
For a distinctive taste, you may make
the syrup by replacing the sugar with
grape molasses in step 1 as follows:

1 cup grape molasses
1/2 cup water
1/2 cup rosewater
1 tablespoon lime juice

1. Make the syrup: Combine the sugar and water in a saucepan, and stir well to dissolve the sugar. Bring to a boil and add the rosewater and lime juice. Remove from heat and set aside to cool.

2. Make the filling: In a large mixing bowl, blend together the almonds, sugar and cardamom. Set aside.

3. Make the dough: In a mixing bowl or food processor, mix the milk, oil, 1 tablespoon cooled syrup, rosewater and egg.

4. Stir in the flour to form a dough. Knead the dough for 5 to 10 minutes, until it no longer sticks to your fingers. Divide the dough into 2 balls of equal size; enclose each ball in plastic wrap.

5. Grease a 17-by-11-by-1-inch nonstick baking sheet with oil. Preheat the oven to 350°F.

6. Dust a large, flat work surface with flour. Roll out 1 ball of dough and use a long, narrow rolling pin to roll it into a sheet 1 inch larger all around than the baking sheet.

7. Roll the dough around the rolling pin; unroll it over the baking sheet, allowing the excess to overlap the sheet.

8. Spread the filling over the dough sheet, pressing down with your hands to make a firm, even layer. This simplifies cutting the baklava later.

9. Roll out the second ball of dough as you did the first, and transfer over the top of the filling. With your hands, press the dough down to form an even layer.

10. Pinch the overhanging top and bottom edges of dough together to seal them, forming a rim around the edges of the baklava.

11. With a sharp knife and a ruler as a guide, cut through the top layer of the baklava diagonally in a cross-hatch pattern to create diamond shapes 1 inch wide.

12. Brush the dough all over with the remaining oil. Place the baking sheet in the middle of the preheated oven.

13. Bake for 30 to 35 minutes, until the baklava turns pink. Remove it from the oven and pour 2/3 of the syrup evenly over the top (keep the rest for later use, if needed).

14. Decorate the baklava with the pistachios and rose petals. Cover it tightly with aluminum foil and let it rest for 2 to 24 hours.

15. Use a sharp knife to cut and lift the diamond shaped pieces onto a serving platter. To store, cover tightly with plastic wrap and refrigerate for as long as 3 weeks, or freeze for as long as 3 months.

Serving Note

Can be included in a chef's plate, served with Najmieh's Tea (see page 228).

Wine Note

Baklava goes well with wine; the spicy pistachios and perfumed rosewater are made for dessert. Pair with a late-harvest to bring out the floral notes, or with darker sweet wines such as a Late Bottled Vintage Port, Pedro Ximenez Sherry or Malmsey Madeira to amplify the caramel-nut tones. Though each sweet wine has its own voice, all are in tune with the baklava.

Chickpea Cookies

Nan-e nokhodchi

Makes: 40 pieces
Preparation time: 30 minutes
Cooking time: 30 minutes

1 cup canola oil
1 1/2 cups confectioners' sugar
4 teaspoons ground cardamom
1 tablespoon rosewater
3 to 3 1/2 cups roasted chickpea
  flour (fine), triple-sifted

Garnish
4 tablespoons unsalted, slivered
  pistachios

Variation
You may replace the 1 1/2 cups sugar
with 1/2 cup confectioners' sugar and
1/2 cup grape molasses.

Note
It is important to use the fine
chickpea flour intended for pastry and
not the coarser flour used for savory
dishes.

1. In a mixing bowl combine oil, sugar, cardamom and rosewater, and mix for 2 minutes until creamy. Add 3 cups chickpea flour and mix for 1 minute until dough is no longer sticky.

2. Dust work surface with chickpea flour and knead the dough. Add more chickpea flour if needed. Flatten the dough to 6 inches square and 3/4 inch thick. Wrap in plastic wrap and allow to rest for 1 to 24 hours in the refrigerator. The resulting cool, flat dough will be easier to cut.

3. Preheat the oven to 300°F. Line a baking sheet with a nonstick baking mat. Remove dough from wrapper and unroll. Use a cloverleaf cookie cutter to cut clover shapes out of the dough. Place these on the baking mat, leaving 1 inch between each one to allow their expansion when cooked, and decorate each one in its center with a slivered pistachio. Place baking sheet on the center rack of the oven.

4. Bake for 25 to 30 minutes, or until the cookies' bases show a light, golden color. Remove cookies from oven and **allow to cool.**

5. Carefully lift cookies off the baking mat (these cookies crumble very easily). Store in an airtight container and keep in a cool place.

A Persian silver-gilded
decanter from the sixth
century depicting a
vintaging scene.

Raisin Cookies

Nan-e keshmeshy

Makes: 30 cookies
Preparation time: 15 minutes
Cooking time: 10 to 15 minutes

1 cup (2 sticks) unsalted
  butter, softened
1 teaspoon vanilla extract
1 3/4 cups sugar
4 large eggs
2 cups raisins
2 1/3 cups unbleached
  all-purpose flour

1. Preheat the oven to 350°F. Line a cookie sheet with a baking mat.

2. In a large mixing bowl whisk the butter, vanilla extract and sugar until smooth. Then whisk in the eggs one at a time. Stir until the mixture is creamy.

3. Stir in the raisins.

4. Add the flour. Then, with a rubber spatula, fold in the flour until a soft dough forms.

5. Using a small ice-cream scoop, pick up a scoop full of the dough and place mounds onto the cookie sheet lined with a baking mat, leaving about 2 inches between each scoop.

6. Place the baking sheet in the center of the preheated oven and bake for 10 minutes or until the cookies are golden brown.

7. Remove the cookies from the oven and immediately loosen them from the mat with a flat spatula: Keep in mind cooled raisin cookies will stick to the mat.

8. Transfer the raisin cookies to a serving platter. To store, place them in an airtight plastic container and refrigerate until ready to serve.

Quince Baked in Pomegranate Juice & Grape Molasses

Moraba-ye beh ba anar

Servings: 4
Preparation time: 15 minutes
Cooking time: 4 hours

Syrup
3 cups pomegranate juice
1/2 cup grape molasses
3/4 cup sugar
1 vanilla bean, split and scraped out,
  or 1/2 teaspoon vanilla extract
1 tablespoon fresh lime juice
2 medium-sized quinces
4 cinnamon sticks (3 inches each)
4 bay leaves

Garnish
Vanilla ice cream or frozen yogurt
  (optional)
1/2 cup fresh pomegranate seeds or
  raisins
1/2 cup toasted walnuts, chopped
  (optional)

1. Preheat oven to 350°F.

2. In a mixing bowl, combine the pomegranate juice, grape molasses, sugar, vanilla and lime juice, and stir well.

3. Wash and peel the quinces; core them and cut into halves.

4. Place the quince halves face up in a deep baking dish large enough for the 4 half quinces.

5. Lay a cinnamon stick and a bay leaf inside the hollow of each quince.

6. Dribble the syrup over the quinces, cover and bake for 3 hours, basting occasionally, until the quinces are pinkish-red. Uncover and continue to bake for another hour, until red.

7. Remove from the oven and transfer to individual serving dishes.

Serving Note

Place a half of quince in a serving dish with vanilla ice cream or frozen yogurt on top. Garnish with pomegranate seeds and chopped walnuts.

Wine Note

Rich and earthy, quince pairs best with a late-harvest red such as Zinfandel or Grenache. A sweet sherry will also pair well.

Servings: 4
Preparation time: 20 minutes, plus
  30 minutes refrigeration

1 cup pomegranate seeds (about 1
  pomegranate)
6 large oranges, peeled and sliced
  (with membrane removed), chilled
1/4 cup candied orange rind (recipe
  below)
1/2 cup fresh orange juice
1 tablespoon fresh squeezed
  lime juice
1 teaspoon orange blossom water

Garnish
6 organic orange blossoms (optional)
6 organic orange leaves (optional)

Servings: 8
Preparation time: 5 minutes
Cooking time: 1 hour 30 minutes

Candied Orange Rind
1 cup orange rind (about 5 oranges),
  chopped and rinsed
1 1/2 cups orange juice (about 3
  oranges)
1 cup sugar
1 tablespoon cooking orange blossom
  water

Saffron Pudding
1 cup white short-grain rice
7 cups water
1/2 teaspoon salt
1 cup sugar or grape molasses
1/2 cup unsalted butter
1/2 cup unsalted slivered almonds
1/2 teaspoon ground saffron,
  dissolved in 2 tablespoons hot water
1/2 teaspoon ground cardamom
1/2 cup rosewater

Garnish
2 teaspoons ground cinnamon
2 teaspoons slivered almonds
2 teaspoons slivered pistachios

Pomegranate & Orange Fruit Salad

Deser-e anar-o porteqal

In a glass bowl or container, combine the pomegranate seeds, orange segments, candied orange rind, orange juice, lime juice and orange blossom water. Cover and chill in the refrigerator for at least 30 minutes.

Serving Note

Serve chilled in individual dishes, and garnish with an orange blossom and an orange leaf.

Wine Note

Enjoy this vibrant fresh fruit dessert when the citrus crop is at its best. Oranges go well with sweet wines. The pomegranate seeds keep this dessert refreshing and zesty. Pair with late-harvest wines, especially those made from the Muscat or Gewurztraminer grape.

Orange Saffron Rice Pudding

Sholeh zard

1. To make the candied orange rind, combine the orange rind, orange juice, sugar and orange blossom water in a small saucepan, and cook over medium heat for 10 minutes.

2. To make the pudding, pick over the rice and rinse in a fine-mesh colander.

3. Combine the rice with 5 cups of water and the salt in a medium-sized saucepan and bring to a boil, skimming the foam as it rises. Cover and simmer for 25 minutes over low heat until the rice is quite soft, stirring occasionally.

4. Add 2 more cups of warm water and the sugar, and cook for 25 minutes longer, stirring occasionally.

5. Add the butter, almonds, saffron water, cardamom and rosewater—plus all the candied orange rind together with its syrup. Stir well. Cover and simmer over low heat for 20 minutes. Remove the cover and cook over low heat, uncovered, for another 5 to 10 minutes or until the mixture has thickened to a pudding.

Serving Note

Spoon the hot pudding into individual serving bowls. Garnish and keep chilled.

Pomegranate Jelly

Jeleh-ye anar

Servings: 6
Preparation time: 15 minutes
Setting time: 8 hours

4 envelopes unflavored gelatin
4 cups freshly squeezed or
  bottled pomegranate juice
2 tablespoons grape molasses
  or honey (if pomegranates are
  too sour)
Seeds of 4 fresh pomegranates

1. In a large bowl, dissolve the unflavored gelatin in 1 cup of cold pomegranate juice. Let stand for 1 minute.

2. In a saucepan, warm 3 cups of pomegranate juice.

3. Add the softened gelatin to the saucepan. Stir constantly for 5 minutes.

4. Taste it. If too sour, add grape molasses to taste. Pour the pomegranate juice mixture into individual bowls.

5. Scatter the pomegranate seeds on top. Chill it in the refrigerator until firm (about 8 hours).

Figs Caramelized in Grape Sauce

Compot-e anjir

Makes: 4 half-pint jars
Preparation time: 5 minutes
Cooking time: 15 minutes

2 pounds green or yellow figs (firm, seedless and fresh)
1 cup grape molasses
1/2 cup water
2 green cardamom pods, crushed
1 cinnamon stick (4 inches)
1 vanilla bean or 1/2 teaspoon vanilla extract
1 tablespoon lime juice

1. Wash the figs. Do not remove the stem.

2. Place the grape molasses, water, cardamom, cinnamon and vanilla in a laminated pot, and bring to a boil. Reduce heat, cover and simmer for about 10 to 15 minutes over medium heat, or until the figs have caramelized. Add the lime juice and simmer for 2 minutes longer. Remove from heat.

Serving Note

Serve with drained yogurt, or fresh cream, or ice cream. Garnish with mint sprigs.

Rose & Nightingale Saffron & Pistachio Ice Cream

Bastani-e gol-e bolbol

Servings: 4
Preparation time: 25 minutes
Freezing time: 3 hours

1 cup whipping cream
3 tablespoons Cortas sahlab mixture
 (available in Iranian groceries) or
 1 tablespoon pure ground sahlab
 (harder to find)
4 cups milk
1 cup sugar or grape molasses
1/4 teaspoon salt
1/4 teaspoon ground saffron threads,
 dissolved in 1 tablespoon hot water
2 tablespoons cooking rosewater
1/2 teaspoon mastic ground with 1
 teaspoon sugar
1/4 cup unsalted pistachios, shelled

Garnish
8 three-inch-round ice-cream wafers
1 teaspoon grape molasses (optional)

Note
To make the ice cream in wafers as
shown in the photograph, spread the
ice cream (from the machine) on
an 8 x 10-inch wafer sheet, place
another wafer sheet on top, wrap in
shrinkwrap and place in the freezer.
When fully refrozen, use a sharp knife
to cut the ice cream wafer sheets
into wedge shapes, or according to
your fancy.

1. Pour the whipping cream into a 9-inch freezer-proof pie dish and place in the freezer.

2. In a small bowl, dissolve the sahlab mixture in 1 cup cold milk until quite smooth. Set aside.

3. In a medium saucepan, bring 3 cups milk and the sugar to a boil, then reduce heat to very low. Add the sahlab-milk mixture, salt, saffron, rosewater and mastic, and bring back to a boil. Reduce heat to low and simmer, whisking constantly, for 10 to 20 minutes, until thick enough for the mixture to coat the back of a spoon. Remove from heat and allow to cool to room temperature. Chill in the refrigerator (about 1 hour). Pour into a chilled ice-cream maker and follow the manufacturer's instructions for making ice cream.

4. Pour the ice cream into a plastic container with a press-in-place lid. Remove the whipping cream from the freezer. Remove it from the pan and break it into 1/4-inch pieces. With a rubber spatula fold it into the ice cream. Add the pistachios and continue to fold for another 20 seconds.

5. Cover tightly (uncovered ice cream develops an unpleasant taste). Freeze the ice cream for at least 1 hour to allow it to develop texture and flavor.

6. Twenty minutes before serving, remove the ice cream from the freezer and refrigerate.

Serving Note

Serve by placing between two wafers, or place a scoop of ice cream on a plate and garnish with grape molasses and a wafer.

Wine Note

Creamy, sweet and full of yellow saffron spice, this is an exotic ice cream that satisfies on its own or with a few butter cookies. But it is amazing with a late-harvest wine. The sweet golden wine, especially one aged in new oak barrels, pairs quite well with the saffron spice and creamy texture of this dessert.

Rice Noodle Sorbet with Grape Molasses

Paludeh-ye shirazi

Servings: 6
Preparation time: 15 minutes
Cooking time: 5 minutes
Setting time: 1 hour

2 1/2 cups water
2 cups sugar
4 ounces thin rice-stick noodles
 or rice vermicelli, snipped, with
 scissors, into 3-inch lengths, soaked
 in warm water for 30 minutes and
 drained
1/4 teaspoon salt
2 tablespoons light corn syrup
1/4 cup fresh lime juice
1 tablespoon cooking rosewater

Garnish
2 tablespoons pistachios
1/4 cup grape molasses or fresh
 blackberries
4 tablespoons fresh lime juice

1. Bring 8 cups of water to a boil and drop in the noodles. Boil for 5 minutes, drain and rinse in cold water.

2. In a saucepan, combine the water and sugar and bring to a boil. Remove from heat. Add all remaining ingredients, except the noodles, and stir well. Allow to cool.

3. Pour the mixture into an ice-cream maker and start the machine. When the mixture turns from an opaque color to a white, frozen, icy consistency, begin adding the noodles, a little at a time, allowing them to freeze before adding the next batch (this stage is important—the mixture has to have an icy consistency before adding the noodles, and the noodles have to be added gradually to have a chance to be frozen). When the noodles freeze properly, they will not have a rubbery texture.

Serving Note

Scoop some sorbet into individual sorbet dishes and garnish with pistachios, grape molasses and lime juice.

WINE TO SHERBET

With the advent of Islam, Iranians generally discarded the old Persian words for wine (badeh *and* mey) *and replaced them with* sharab, *Arabic for "sweet drink." That is the source of the English "syrup."*

But renaming the forbidden was not enough. They needed a new name for their nonalcoholic drink, and sharbat *was born. Its basis was the ice and snow that Iranians had learned to preserve during the hot summer months in spectacular domed ice wells on the edges of towns and along caravan routes. The flavorings were syrups, made by combining fruit or vegetable juice with honey, sugar, or date or grape molasses and boiling the mixture down to intensify the flavor. Sipped through a mound of crushed ice or snow, the syrup became a delightful drink.*

Sharbats *could be either sweet or savory. The Huguenot jeweler Jean Chardin, traveling in Iran, described a favorite of the Isfahanis: sugar, a pinch of salt, lemon or pomegranate juice, and a squeeze of garlic or lemon, all mixed with crushed ice. This sweet-sour mixture, he found, not only quenched the thirst but stimulated the appetite.*

Such cool drinks traveled along the trade routes to become the sharbats *of Turkey and Syria, the* sorbete *of Spain, the* sorbeto *of Italy, the* sorbet *of France and the sherbet of England. The European versions were iced mixtures, usually based on fruit, that one ate with a spoon—merely a difference in the degree of freezing.*

Such frozen desserts in Iran are made with lime juice, sour cherries or black mulberries and served with sweet rice vermicelli. They have their own name: paludeh *or* faludeh. *A Persian* sharbat *remains a fruit drink with plenty of ice, often perfumed with rosewater or orange blossoms and served in summer.*

𝒲ine Note

A delicate dessert; pair with a sparkling Muscato d'Asti or a
late-harvest Viognier.

Pomegranate Granita

Bastani-e anar

Servings: 6
Preparation time: 15 minutes
Setting time: 4 hours

4 cups bottled pomegranate juice (or the juice of 8 medium-sized fresh pomegranates)
1/2 cup sugar
2 tablespoons fresh lime juice
1 cup pomegranate arils (about 2 pomegranates)
2 tablespoons light corn syrup
1 tablespoon grape molasses

1. Mix all the ingredients with a rubber spatula until the sugar has dissolved.

2. Pour the mixture into a wide container and place in the freezer, uncovered. Leave for 2 hours. Break up the frozen juice with a fork and return to the freezer for another hour. Repeat this one more time or until it forms into a granita.

Serving Note

Serve the granita either in emptied out, frozen pomegranate shells or in individual serving dishes. Garnish with fresh arils when in season.

Wine Note

Icy, sweet and tangy, this is a very refreshing ice. It goes well with a late-harvest wine but will also pair nicely with a port, sweet sherry or Madeira. Ices are not usually right with wine because of their coldness and high sugar content, but this one works.

Three Sherbets

Vinegar & Mint Sherbet

Sharbat-e sekanjebin

1. Bring the sugar and water to a boil in a medium saucepan. Simmer for 10 minutes over medium heat, stirring occasionally, until sugar has thoroughly dissolved.

2. Add the vinegar and boil for 15 to 20 minutes over medium heat, until a thick syrup forms. Remove the saucepan from the heat.

3. Wash 4 mint sprigs, pat dry and add them to the syrup. Allow to cool. Remove the mint and pour the syrup into a clean, dry bottle. Cork tightly.

Serving Note

These 3 sherbets can also be served together in cocktail glasses as chilled desserts. In individual glasses mix 1 part syrup with 3 parts water, crushed ice, 4 cucumber slices, 2 lime slices, 1 sprig of fresh mint and 1 sprig lemon verbena. Stir well with a tall spoon. Serve well chilled.

Tart Cherry Sherbet

Sharbat-e Albalu

1. Squeeze the cherries or process them in a juicer.

2. Bring the sugar, lime juice and water to a boil in a laminated pan. Add the cherry juice and boil for 10 to 15 minutes over medium heat, stirring occasionally, until the syrup thickens.

3. Remove the pan from the heat and allow to cool.

Serving Note

In a tall glass, mix 1 part syrup, 3 parts water and crushed ice for each person. Stir with a spoon and top with fresh cherries.

Apple & Rosewater Sherbet

In a pitcher, mix the sugar, water and rosewater. Stir well with a spoon until the sugar has dissolved completely.

Serving Note

Add some grated apple and crushed ice to individual glasses, and pour in the sherbet.

Makes: 1 pint
Preparation time: 10 minutes
Cooking time: 30 minutes

6 cups sugar
2 cups water
1 1/2 cups wine vinegar
4 sprigs fresh mint

Garnish
1 cucumber, peeled and
  sliced thinly
2 limes, thinly sliced
4 sprigs fresh mint
4 sprigs lemon verbena

Makes: 1 pint
Preparation time: 20 minutes
Cooking time: 15 minutes

3 pounds fresh or frozen
  pitted sour cherries (about 3
  cups of sour-cherry juice)
6 cups sugar
4 tablespoons lime juice
3 cups water

Servings: 4
Preparation time: 15 minutes
Cooking time: none

1/2 cup sugar
4 cups ice water
1 teaspoon rosewater
4 crisp apples, cored, peeled
  and coarsely grated

Najmieh's Tea
Chai-ye najmieh

1. Bring water to a boil in a tea kettle. Warm a teapot by swirling some boiling water in it; pour out the water. Place 2 tablespoons of Persian tea leaves in the pot, using perfumed Ghazal or any black tea from a Persian store, and 2 tablespoons of orange blossom water to get the effect of Persian tea (the color and aroma of this tea will be delightful).

2. Fill the teapot half full with boiling water. Replace the lid, cover the pot with a cozy and let the tea steep for 5 to 10 minutes. Do not steep for more than 10 minutes: The quality will deteriorate and you will have to start over. If you are using a samovar, steep the tea on top.

3. Pour a glassful of tea and return it to the pot to make sure the tea is evenly mixed.

4. Fill each glass or cup halfway with tea. Add boiling water from the kettle to dilute the tea to the desired color and taste: Some prefer their tea weak, some strong. Keep the pot covered with the cozy while you drink the first glasses.

Najmieh's Coffee
Qahveh-ye najmieh

For each small cup (4 ounces—demitasse or espresso), put 1 teaspoon of powdered coffee (very, very finely ground, available at Persian grocery stores), 1 teaspoon of sugar, a dash of ground cardamom and saffron, and 1 cup of water (4 ounces) into a small pan or ibrik. Stir with a spoon. Simmer over low heat until foam rises to the surface. Remove from the heat and stir until the foam subsides. Repeat this process 2 more times (don't walk away; this coffee needs supervision). To make sure that every cup of coffee has the same consistency, fill each cup a little at a time, until each is full. Sip the coffee carefully so as not to swallow any grounds.

After drinking this coffee, remove the saucer and place it on top of the cup. Invert the cup and saucer away from yourself with your left hand (the hand of the heart) and make a wish as you do so. A fortune teller—or just an insightful friend—can read your fate in the pattern of the grounds left behind in the cup.

Rosebud Tea

Chai-e gol

Servings: 4 cups   Preparation time: 20 minutes
4 cups water, 1 tablespoon organic rose buds

Bring the water to a boil in a kettle. Add the rose buds to a see-through glass teapot. Add the boiling water. Cover and steep for 20 minutes on top of a samovar or simmering kettle or by using a tea cozy. Bring the teapot to the table, along with a small glass and bowl of sugar on a small tray for each individual. Fill each glass with tea. Leave the teapot on the table and cover it with a tea cozy.

Mint Tea

Chai-e Na'na

Servings: 4 cups   Preparation time: 20 minutes
4 cups water, 1 cup fresh mint

Bring the water to a boil in a kettle. Add the mint to a see-through glass teapot. Add the boiling water. Cover and steep for 20 minutes on top of a samovar or simmering kettle or by using a tea cozy. Bring the teapot to the table, along with a small glass and bowl of sugar on a small tray for each individual. Fill each glass with tea. Leave the teapot on the table and cover it with a tea cozy.

Note
You can replace the mint with lemon verbina.

Saffron Tea

Chai-e Zaferun

Servings: 4 cups   Preparation time: 20 minutes
4 cups water, 1/2 teaspoon saffron threads, 1/2 teaspoon sugar or honey

Bring the water to a boil in a saucepan. Add the saffron and sugar to a see-through glass teapot. Add the boiling water. Cover and steep for 20 minutes on top of a samovar or simmering kettle or by using a tea cozy. Bring the teapot to the table, along with a small glass and bowl of sugar on a small tray for each individual. Fill each glass with tea. Leave the teapot on the table and cover it with a tea cozy.

THE CULTURE OF HOSPITALITY

The Persian culture of hospitality is very old and has touched everyone who has experienced it. The excerpts below, wonderfully translated by Reuben Levy, are by Amir Kaykavus, an eleventh-century Persian prince from Gorgan who wrote an entire book to guide his favorite son in avoiding the pitfalls of life. One section is about proper conduct when his son entertains guests or is a guest himself. In the pages that follow, I have listed my own suggestions and some menus for successfully entertaining in the Persian way in the twenty-first century.

◆ MY SON, do not offer hospitality to strangers every day, for you cannot constantly provide it in worthy fashion. Observe on how many occasions each month you have guests at your table, then reduce them from five to one, expending on that one occasion what previously you have spent on five. Thereby your table will be freed from defects and the tongues of cavilers will be stilled.

◆ WHEN GUESTS come to visit you, go out to welcome each one and pay him your respects, giving them severally the honors which are their due.

◆ DO NOT apologize to your guests (it is the habit of tradesmen), and do not continually be saying, "Eat well," or "You are eating nothing; I pray you not to be modest," or "I, for my part, cannot provide you with anything worthy of you, but next time something better will be provided." Expressions of that kind are not used by persons of distinction.

◆ IN THE room where you assemble, have herbs in abundance and engage sweet-voiced and expert minstrels to be present. Unless the wine is good, do not place it before your guests; it is a daily experience for men to eat, and in consequence the wine and music should be good, so that if there are any shortcomings at table or in the dishes provided, they will be covered by the wine and the music.

◆ EVEN IF you have performed toward your guests all the duties I have mentioned, do not regard them as being under any obligation to you, considering, rather, that they have many claims upon you.

◆ YOU MUST be grateful to your guests and show them a pleasant face. But be sparing in your wine drinking and never present yourself before your guests in a state of intoxication. Only when you have ascertained that the company has reached a state of semi-intoxication should you begin to put yourself into the same state. First drink a toast to your friends, then pleasantly and cheerfully drink and pass the wine. But do not indulge in foolish laughter over nothing. Foolish laughter is a form of lunacy, just as much as laughing too little is a form of excessive solemnity.

◆ IF YOUR servants commit some fault, overlook it and do not show a sour visage in front of your invited company; also begin no quarrel with your servants by declaring one thing good and another bad. If something fails to please you, order them not to do it again, but tolerate it for that once.

◆ AS FOR your guest, even if he says and does a thousand foolish things, never take him to task for it, but treat him with great regard.

◆ NOW ALTHOUGH hospitality is a duty, the hospitality which is worthy of recognition is not such as to require you to invite any undesirable person into your house, and then to make a show of humility by saying, "This is my guest." You must be discriminating in your choice of the persons to whom you offer this generosity and friendliness.

◆ IF YOU go as a guest, let it not be to all and sundry; it would be derogatory to your prestige. When you go, do not be in a state of great hunger nor yet completely satiated; for if you eat nothing your host will be offended, and if you eat to excess it would be inelegant.

◆ WHEN YOU go into your host's dwelling, sit where you are put and in what is your proper place. Even though it be the house of a familiar friend and you have business there, do not play the master at table or over the wine, and do not give orders to your host's servants, saying, "So-and-so, place that tray here and carry that dish there," giving it to be understood that you are a member of the household.

◆ FURTHER, do not be over officious as a guest, concerning yourself too familiarly with the bread and food of the company; and do not give your servant food from the table for him to carry away.

◆ NEVER PERMIT yourself to be completely overcome by wine, but rise in such condition that the signs of drunkenness will not be apparent in you. Drunkenness should not take possession of you to the extent that you lose the semblance of humanity, and practice all your drunkenness at home.

◆ EXCESSIVE TALK (during intoxication) is a sign of drunkenness; so also are excessive hand-clapping, the stamping of feet and unnecessary displays of affection. Whether drunk or sober, hereafter guard against any of the things which I have described as drunken conduct. Never appear before any stranger in a state of intoxication nor indeed before anyone except your own family or servants. Do not demand that all the music performed by the minstrels shall be in light modes, otherwise you will be charged with levity and frivolousness. Yet most young men demand the light or the sorrowful modes.

PLANNING A PERSIAN-STYLE DINNER

Persian food offers a palette of almost limitless possibilities, whether for a big dinner party or an intimate gathering of family and friends. Whatever the occasion, you have plenty of scope for creativity and surprise.

In the following seven menus, I have brought together some widely varied tastes and textures for the seasons as well as for Sunday brunch, the New Year meal, and the *Sizdehbedar* picnic. These menus are intended to give you a pleasing, unified meal, especially when accompanied by good wine. I have not provided many variations, leaving it up to you to mix and match as you please.

Planning is the most important element for a peaceful and enjoyable dinner. Make sure your partner, your children, your helpers all know what is expected of them: who will be cooking, who will do the shopping, who will serve the drinks, who will set the table, who will assign seats, who will take care of the children if necessary and so on. If you have very young children, make it clear who will be taking care of them should something come up. If they are older, I encourage you to include them whenever possible. (I have found that if they are given the option of being included at the table, they will generally satisfy their curiosity and then go to bed or otherwise occupy themselves. If they are strictly excluded you will pay in other ways.) Plan on having everything ready an hour before your guests are to arrive, then relax with your companion and children, have a drink and taste the food you have prepared.

Keep in mind that the purpose of any social gathering is enjoyment—not a performance or a competition to outdo others. No matter how hard you have worked or how much more there is to do, you must be grateful to your guests and show them that you are happy to see them. If you are behind schedule or things don't go as planned when your guests arrive, don't panic: Be flexible and involve them so they can help. If, for example, your companion is late and cannot serve the drinks, ask one of the guests to be the *saqi*. Being relaxed and having a pleasant face is the key to entertaining. You should welcome each of your guests personally and introduce them to anyone they may not know. Never let them feel neglected. Don't do what a young couple did when my husband and I were invited to their house for dinner: We were the first guests to arrive, and we were left alone in their very sumptuous living room for about fifteen minutes while the couple fussed in the kitchen. We would have been happier helping them there; or at least one of them should have stayed with us. This is a no-no in the rules of entertaining the Persian way. On another occasion the hosts' two children, who were quite old enough to join us, were eating in the kitchen while we were eating in the dining room at a large table that had plenty of room to include the young ones.

Last but not least, the ingredients that you use should be fresh, seasonal and preferably organic. Cooking for someone is a conveyance of love and energy. One good dish made by you with love is better than a dozen store-bought ones. Finally, the quality of your wine is important. As the Persian Prince Kaykavus advised his son in the eleventh century, "Any shortcomings at the table will be covered by good wine and music." Happy cooking and *nush-e jan.*

SUNDAY MENU

HORS D'OEUVRES

Bread, Goat Cheese, Herbs, Nuts & Grapes
NAN-O PANIR-O SABZI KHORDAN BA ANGUR

OR

Spicy Lamb Turnover
SANBOUSEH

SOUP

Noodle Soup with Verjuice
ASH-E RESHTEH BA AB GHUREH

OR

Barley & Leek Soup
SUP-E JO

MAIN COURSE

*Veal Fillet Kebab in Saffron & Roses & Ground Lamb Kebab
with Shallot Sauce on Lavash Bread, a Bowl of Fresh Persian Basil
and Shirazi-Style Salad on the Side*
KABAB-E SHAHNAMEH VA KABAB-E KUBIDEH BA NAN-E LAVASH-O RAYHUN-O SALAD SHIRAZI

OR

*Chicken Kebab with Shallot Sauce on Lavash Bread, a Bowl of Fresh
Persian Basil & Shirazi-Style Salad on the Side*
JUJEH KABAB BA NAN-E LAVASH-O RAYHUN-O SALAD SHIIRAZI

OR

*Sturgeon Kebab with Grape Sauce & Saffron Steamed Rice with
Four-Hearts Green Salad on the Side*
KABAB-E UZUNBURUN BA SHIREH-YE ANGUR-O KATEH BA SALAD-E CHAHAR MAGHZ

DESSERT

Pomegranate Granita
BASTANI-E ANAR

OR

Pomegranate Jelly
JELLEH-YE ANAR

Najmieh's Tea Served with Raisin Cookies
CHAI-E NAJMIEH BA NAN-E KESHMESHI

Spring Menu

HORS D'OEUVRES

Feta Goat Cheese, Walnuts & Fresh Herbs Green Bites on Cucumber

DOUGMAJ: LOGHMEH-YE SABZ-E ESHQABAD

OR

Fava Beans with Angelica

BAQALA POKHTEH

APPETIZER

Vine Leaf Wrapped Lamb Kebab

KABAB-E BARG-E MO BA SHIREH-YE ANGUR

SOUP

Chilled Yogurt Soup with Rose Petals, Raisins &
Flat Bread Croutons

ABDUGH KHIAR BA TILIT

OR

Barley & Leek Soup

SUP-E JO

MAIN COURSE

Spring-Lamb Shank Braise in Merlot, Saffron & Rosewater with Fava
Bean & Dill Steamed Rice with Lavash Crust with
Pickled Garlic & Drained Yogurt

BAQALA POLOW BA MAHICHEH-YE BARREH

OR

Catfish with Sumac & Mung Bean & Dill Bulgur

MAHI-O SUMAQ BA DAMI-E BALGHUR

SALAD

Four-Hearts Green Salad: Romaine Lettuce, Caramelized Pistachios
Hazelnuts & Almonds Served with an Aromatic Vinaigrette

SALAD-E CHAHAR MAGHZ

DESSERT

Platter of Pomegranate Granita, Rice Noodle Sorbet, &
Rose & Nightingale Saffron Pistachio Ice Cream

DORIEH-YE BASTANI-E ANAR, FALUDEH VA BASTANI-E GOL-O BOLBOL

Najmieh's Tea Served with Baklava

CHAI-E NAJMIEH BA BAQLAVA

Summer Menu

Cracked Wheat & Lentil Bites

TARKHINEH-YE ADAS

Grilled Eggplant with Sun-Dried Yogurt, Dates & Mint Fries

KASHK-E BADEMJAN

Tamarind & Kholrabi Soup

ASH-E PARSY-E NARGIL-O TAMR-E HENDI

*Pan-Roasted Quail or Game Hen Infused with Verjuice with Tart
Cherry Rice & Lamb Meatballs under a Lavash Bread Crust*

ALBALU POLOW BA KUFTEH-O BELDERCHIN

OR

*Chicken Apricot & Rice in Pastry with
Yogurt & Saffron-Infused Chicken Braise*

PLOW DAR NAN-E LAVASH BA KHORESH-E MAST-O ZAFERUN

Peach Salad with Walnuts Caramelized in Grape Molasses

SALAD-E HULU BA GERDU-YE SUKHTEH

Three Sherbets: Vinegar, Cherry & Apple

SEH SHARBAT-E SEKANJEBIN, ALBALU VA FALUDEH-YE SIB

Najmieh's Tea Served with Baklava

CHAI-E NAJMIEH BA BAQLAVA

AUTUMN MENU

HORS D'OEUVRES

Caspian Olive Tapenade

ZEYTOUN PARVARDEH

APPETIZER

Split Pea Patties with Quince

SHAMI-E LAPEH

SOUP

Pistachio Soup

SUP-E PESTEH

MAIN COURSE

Roast Pheasant with Caramelized Quince Braise

POLOW KHORESH-E BEH BA QARQAVOL

OR

*Lamb Shank & Aromatic Herbs with Red Beans & Dried Lime Braise
on Steamed Rice Crust*

KHORESH-E QORMEH SABZI BA CHELOW

OR

Saffron Chicken, Eggplant & Barberry Rice Cake

SHIRAZI POLO-YE QALEBI

SALAD

Tribal Cucumber Salad

SALAD-E ANAR-O KHIAR

DESSERT

Pomegranate Granita

BASTANI-E ANAR

Najmieh's Tea Served with Baklava

CHAI-E NAJMIEH BA BAQLAVA

WINTER MENU

HORS D'OEUVRES

Lamb Liver Kebab
KABAB-E JIGAR

OR

Feta Goat Cheese, Walnuts & Fresh Herbs Green Bites on Cucumber
DOUGMAJ: LOGHMEH-YE SABZ-E ESHQABAD

APPETIZER

Pomegranate & Pistachio Meatballs
KUFTEH-YE ANAR

SOUP

Barley & Leek Soup
SUP-E JOW

MAIN COURSE

Persian Gulf-Style Striped Bass & Shrimp Braise with Tamarind
QALIYEH-YE MAHI-O MEYGU

OR

Duck Braise in Merlot & Pomegranate on Wedding Rice
SHIRIN POLOW BA ORDAK

SALAD

Four-Hearts Green Salad: Romaine Lettuce, Caramelized Pistachios
Hazelnuts & Almonds Served with an Aromatic Vinaigrette
SALAD-E CHAHAR MAGHZ

DESSERT

Quince Baked in Pomegranate Juice & Grape Sauce
MORABA-YE BEH BA ANAR

Najmieh's Tea Served with Chickpea Florets
CHAI-E NAJMIEH BA NAN-E NOKHODCHI

New Year Celebration Menu

MEHMANI-E JASHN-E NOWRUZ

The traditional menu for the Nowruz feast on the first day of spring usually includes fish, eggs, nuts, herbs, noodles & sweets. It is believed these will bring good luck, fertility & prosperity in the year that lies ahead.

PASS AROUND HORS D'OEUVRES

Caviar Canapés; Green Bites; Three Vegetable Yogurt Salads: Spinach, White Bean & Eggplant; Spicy Lamb Turnovers; Split Pea Patties with Quince; Caspian Olive Tapenade; Fava Beans with Angelica

APPETIZER

Pomegranate & Pistachio Meatballs

KUFTEH-YE ANAR

SOUP

Pistachio Soup or Noodle Soup

SUP-E PESTEH YA ASH-E RESHTEH

MAIN COURSE

Sautéd Striped Bass in Bitter Orange & Grape Sauce with Fava Bean & Dill Steamed Rice under Lavash Crust with Fresh Herb Kuku with Barberries

BAQALA POLOW BA MAHI VA NARENJ-O SHIREH-YE ANGUR BA KUKU-YE SABZI OR ZERESHK

SALAD

Four-Hearts Green Salad: Romaine Lettuce, Caramelized Pistachios, Hazelnuts & Almonds Served with an Aromatic Vinaigrette

SALAD-E CHAHAR MAGHZ

DESSERT

Chef's Assortment of Persian Sweets: Chickpea Florets, Baklava, Orange Saffron Rice Pudding & Pomegranate Granita Served with Najmieh's Tea

DORYEH-YE GHAGHALILI-E ASHPAZ BASHI BA CHAI-E NAJMIEH

OUTDOOR THIRTEEN PICNIC MENU

SIZDEHBEDARI

The Persian New Year celebrations continue for twelve days after the first day of spring. On the thirteenth day, called Sizdehbedar, entire families leave their home to go on a picnic (Sizdehbedari). There is much singing, dancing, eating and drinking. With this the Nowruz celebrations are completed.

FOR THE PICNIC BASKET AND THE GRILL

Cauliflower Kuku
KUKU-YE GOL-E KALAM

OR

Fresh Herb Kuku with Bread
KUKU SABZI BA NAN

Noodle Soup
ASH-E RESHTEH

Chicken Kebab
JUJEH KABAB

Lamb Kebab with Pomegranate Glaze
CHENJEH KABAB-E ANAR

Lamb Rib Chops
SHISHLIK-E NEYSHAPOURI

Veal Filet Kebab in Saffron & Roses
KABAB-E SHAHNAMEH

Cucumber & Yogurt with Mint & Rose Petals Salad
BORANI-E KHIAR

Shirazi-Style Cucumber & Tomato Salad
SALAD-E SHIRAZ

Orange Saffron Rice Pudding
SHOLEH ZARD

Mint Tea Served with Raisin Cookies
CHAI-E N'NA BA NAN-E KESHMESH

WHOEVER DESPAIRS

Plant friendship's tree – the heart's desire
    Is the fruit it bears;

And uproot enmity – which only brings
    Sorrows and cares.

Be friendly, easy, with drunkards –
    Good fellowship's theirs;

Since pride brings the hangover, not
    The wineseller's wares.

Talk with your friends, deep in the night,
    And see how life fares

Since when we are gone the heavens
    Will bring others our cares;

And welcome the spring in your heart
    Since the world never spares

To provide for us roses and songbirds,
    Whoever despairs.

And love your beloved – the heavens require you
    To be one who bears

The grief of Majnun all your life:
    God grant me my prayers!

Your heart is so tired! You feel caught
    In the weary world's snares

But sip at the wine, and hear in your heart
    The hope it declares:

That Hafez will sit in his orchard
    By the stream that he shares

With his cypress-slim lover, God willing,
    In the place that is theirs.

Hafez/Davis

درخت دوستی بنشان که کام دل ببار آرد   نهال دشمنی برکن که رنج بی شمار آرد

چو مهمان خراباتی به عزت باش با رندان   که درد سر کشی جانا گرت مستی خمار آرد

شب صحبت غنیمت دان که بعد از روزگار ما   بسی گردش کند گردون بسی لیل و نهار آرد

عماری دار لیلی را که مهد ماه در حکمت   خدا را در دل اندازش که بر مجنون گذار آرد

بهار عمر خواه ای دل وگرنه این چمن هر سال   چو نسرین صد گل آرد بار و چون بلبل هزار آرد

خدا را چون دل ریشم قراری بست با زلفت   بفرما لعل نوشین را که زودش باقرار آرد

درین باغ از خدا خواهد دگر پیر مغان حافظ   نشیند بر لب جویی و سروی در کنار آرد

A detail from a sixteenth-century painting, titled
A Father Advises His Son about Love.

CREDITS

IMAGE PAGES

ii: Prince and Lady under Flowering Branch. Photograph © 2006 Museum of Fine Arts, Boston.

vi: Two Harem Ladies. Photograph © 2006 Royal Asiatic Society, London, England.

1 & 14: Spouted Vessel with Gazelle Protome. Photograph courtesy of Arthur M. Sackler Gallery, Smithsonian Institution, Washington, DC: S1987.33.

2: Abbas 1 and a Saqi. SEF/Art Resources, NY.

4: Wine Cup, Sultan Husayn Mirza Bayqara. Lent by the Art and History Collection, photo © Arthur M. Sackler Gallery Smithsonian Institution, Washington, DC: LTS1995.2.27.

5: Harem of Sultan Husayn Mirza Bayqara. Lent by the Art and History Collection, photo courtesy of the Arthur M. Sackler Gallery, Smithsonian Institution, Washington, DC: LTS1995.2.142.

6–7: Photo, Shiraz Grape Vineyard, Napa Valley. Photo © 2006 Mage Publishers.

8 & 14: Kneeling Bull Holding Spouted Vessel. The Metropolitan Museum of Art, Purchase, Joseph Pulitzer Bequest, 1966 (66.173). Photograph © 1984 The Metropolitan Museum of Art.

9 & 14: Vase in the Shape of a Bird. Photo: Lee Oi-Cheong. Louvre, Paris, France. Réunion des Musées Nationaux/Art Resources, NY. Shiraz Grapes in the Sun, Napa Valley. Photo © 2006 Mage Publishers.

10: The Drunkenness of Noah. Museo dell'Opera del Duomo, Florence, Italy. Photo © 2006 Nicolo Orsi Battaglini/Art Resources, NY.

11: King Jamshid Carried by Divs. Art and History Collection, Arthur M. Sackler Gallery Smithsonian Institution, Washington, DC.

12 & 14: Neolithic wine jar with yellowish residue. University of Pennsylvania Museum (151075 #69-12-15). View of Hajji Firuz Tepe in 1968, structure III, rm 2, with wine jars. Photo © Copyright University of Pennsylvania Museum.

13: View of the foothills of the Zagros Mountains, photo Afshin Bakhtiari. Photo © Copyright 2006 Mage Publishers.

14: Map by Karen E. Rasmussen, Archeographics, Washington, DC. © 2006 Mage Publishers. Map images: Gold cup from Ur; Humpback bull, photos © Copyright The Trustees of The British Museum. Beaker with birds on the rim. The Metropolitan Museum of Art. Gift of Norbert Schimmel Trust, 1989 (1989.281.28). Photograph © 1983 The Metropolitan Museum of Art. Glass blowers guild parade. Photo © Topkapi Palace Museum. All other images credited elsewhere on this page.

17: Greek *Kylix* depicting the voyage of Dionysus. Staatliche Antikensammlungen und Glyptothek Munchen.

18: Detail from *A Fishing Party,* copy of a wall painting from the Tomb of Menna by Davies, Mrs Nina de Garis (1881–1965), Chicago Press, USA. In copyright until 2036.

19: Pottery wine jar with a mud seal. Photo © Copyright The Trustees of The British Museum.

20: Silver Beaker. Photo © Copyright The Trustees of The British Museum. Photo of Cabernet Sauvignon Grapes, Napa Valley. Photo © Copyright 2006 Mage Publishers.

21: Wine Jug. Photo © Copyright The Trustees of The British Museum.

22 & 14: Relief of Ashurbanipal and his queen. Photo © Copyright The Trustees of The British Museum.

24: Carving from Persepolis staircase. Photo © Paul Almasy/Corbis.

25: Persian New Year Setting, photo by Serge Ephraim. Photo © Copyright 2006 Mage Publishers.

26: Elliptical bowl. Freer Gallery of Art, Smithsonian Institution, Washington, DC: Purchase, F1985.28.

27: Rhyton with a ram's head. Haaretz Museum, Tel Aviv, Israel. Photo © Erich Lessing/Art Resources, NY.

28: Spouted vessel in form of a bull. Collection of the Arthur M. Sackler Foundation, NY.

29: Lobed elliptical bowl. Arthur M. Sackler Gallery Smithsonian Institution, Washington, DC: S1987.116. Vessel with two feet. Collection of the Arthur M. Sackler Foundation, NY.

30: Court Musicians. Photo © 2006 Mage Publishers.

31: Kebabs by the fire, photo by Serge Ephraim. Photo © 2006 Mage Publishers.

32: Rhyton with griffin head and forequarters. Photo © Copyright The Trustees of The British Museum.

33: Small bowl inscribed with poetry. Freer Gallery of Art, Smithsonian Institution, Washington, DC: Purchase, F1954.115.

34: Bowl with wheel cut facets. The Metropolitan Museum of Art. Rogers Fund, 1959 (59.34). Photograph © 2000 The Metropolitan Museum of Art.

35: Ewer decorated with female figures. Photograph © Arthur M. Sackler Gallery, Smithsonian Institution, Washington, DC: S1987.117. Chardonnay grapes. Photograph © 2006 Mage Publishers.

36: High-footed bowl with interior medallion. Photograph © Arthur M. Sackler Gallery, Smithsonian Institution, Washington, DC: gift of Arthur M. Sackler S1987.106. Viognier grapes, Napa Valley. Photo © 2006 Mage Publishers.

37: Shirin being shown the portrait of Farhad. By Permission, photo © The British Library.

38: The Garden of Heavenly Creatures. Photograph © Freer Gallery of Art, Smithsonian Institution, Washington, DC: Purchase, F1950.2.

40 Ewer with head of a cock, photo Chuzeville. Réunion des Musées Nationaux/Art Resources, NY. Louvre, Paris, France.

41 Zoomorphic jug with inscription. Photo: M. Beck-Coppola. Musée National de Ceramique, Sevres, France. Réunion des Musées Nationaux/Art Resources, NY.

42: Man filling a wine cup. Freer Gallery of Art, Smithsonian Institution, Washington, DC: Gift of Charles Lang Freer, F1907.2.

44: Rostam kicks aside Bahman's boulder. Photo © The British Library (MSS. 18188/281r).

47: Young man picks grapes in Kholar, Shiraz, photo Afshin Bakhtiari. Photo © 2006 Mage Publishers.

49: Plate from *Voyage du chevalier Chardin en Perse…* (Paris, 1811)

51: Lovers embracing. Photo © Victoria and Albert Museum, London.

53: Coin. Photo © Copyright The Trustees of The British Museum.

54: Heavenly and Earthly Drunkenness, folio from a Divan of Hafez, painted by Sultan Mohammad. Photo by Macintyre, Allan. Courtesy of the Arthur M. Sackler Museum, Harvard University Art Museums, Promised Gift of Mr. and Mrs. Stuart Cary Welch, Jr. Partially owned by the Metropolitan Museum of Art and the Arthur M. Sackler Museum, Harvard University, 1988. In honor of the students of Harvard University and Radcliffe College.

56: Dish with scene of banqueting. Photo © Copyright The Trustees of The British Museum.

57: Khosrow fetes Rostam under the jeweled tree, from the *Shahnameh.* Photo © 2006 Mage Publishers.

58: A picnic at night. Photo © Copyright The Trustees of The British Museum.

60: Ewer. Photograph © Arthur M. Sackler Gallery, Smithsonian Institution, Washington, DC: gift of Arthur M. Sackler S1987.140.

61: Guests of the court of Shah Abbas I. Chehel Sotun Pavilion, Isfahan, Iran. Bridgeman-Giraudon/Art Resources, NY.

63: Anvari Entertains in a Summer House. Arthur M. Sackler Museum, Harvard University, Cambridge, MA.

65: Two Lovers, Reza Abbasi c. 1630. The Metropolitan Museum of Art. Purchase, Francis, M. Weld Gift, 1950 (50.164). Photograph © 1977 The Metropolitan Museum of Art.

66: Star-shaped tile depicting the Simorgh. Photograph © Arthur M. Sackler Gallery, Smithsonian Institution, Washington, DC: gift of Osborne and Gratia Hauge, S1997.114.

68-94: All Darioush Winery photos by Serge Ephraim. Photos © 2006 Mage Publishers.

97: Detail from painting by Esma'il Jallayer. Courtesy of Victoria and Albert Museum, London.

98–241: All food photography by Serge Ephraim. Photos © 2006 Mage Publishers.

142: Firing up the Poet's Kettle. Arthur M. Sackler Museum, Harvard University, Cambridge, MA.

206: Raisins. Photo Afshin Bakhtiari. Photo © 2006 Mage Publishers.

220: Silver gilded vessel. Photo © Copyright The Trustees of The British Museum.

232: Painting by Kamaluddin Behzad (1467–1535). Freer Gallery of Art, Smithsonian Institution, Washington, DC: Purchase, F1944.48.

232: Text from *Qabus Nameh, A Mirror for Princes,* Kai Kavus Ibn Iskandar, translated by Reuben Levy.

242: A father advises his son about love. Freer Gallery of Art, Smithsonian Institution, Washington, DC: Purchase, F1946.12, folio 52a.

246: Panel of tiles (seventeenth century), photo Gerard Blot, Réunion des Musées Nationaux/Art Resources, NY. Louvre, Paris, France.

248: Grapes left to dry, Takestan, Iran. Photo Afshin Bakhtiari. Photo © 2006 Mage Publishers.

254: The Susa Mound, Jules George Bondoux, photo Christian Larrieu, Réunion des Musées Nationaux/Art Resources, NY. Louvre, Paris, France.

POETRY PAGES

v, 64, 243: Khajeh Shamsoddin Mohammad Hafez-Shirazi (c. 1320–1390), couplets translated by Dick Davis.

2, 55, 101, 173: Omar Khayyam (1048–1131), quatrain translated by Edward FitzGerald.

27: Khajeh Shamsoddin Mohammad Hafez-Shirazi (c. 1320–1390), from *Saqi Nameh,* translated by A. J. Arberry.

30, 206: Manuchehri-e Damghani (d. 1041), translated by Dick Davis.

39: Qur'an translations from *The Koran* by N. J. Dawood, Penguin 1974.

39, 70: Jalal al-Din Rumi (1207–1273), from *Masnavi,* translated by Dick Davis.

43: Seyed Hasan Ghaznavi (c. 1150), translated by Dick Davis.

45, 52, 66–67: Abolqasem Ferdowsi (b. 940) from the *Shahnameh,* translated by Dick Davis.

96: Jahan Khatun (fourteenth century), from her *Divan,* translated by Dick Davis.

114: Faghani (fifteenth to sixteenth century), translated by Dick Davis.

165: Khalillullah Khalili (1907–1987), translated by Dick Davis.

246: Fakhruddin Gorgani (1082), from *Vis and Ramin,* translated by Dick Davis.

Persian Calligraphy

Amir Hossein Tabnak

خوشنویسی کتاب توسط امیر حسین تابناک

The shut door meant their hearts could open wide.
With wine the lovers rested from their ride,
Their days now passed in pleasure, and each night
Was filled with joy and mutual delight:
They drank their wine, then lay down face to face,
And drank wine in the midst of their embrace.
Vis like a splendid shining torch now lay
Within her lover's arms till break of day,
And slept till Venus rose, and music woke
Her gently from her sleep, and morning broke:
The last night's wine still lingered in her head
And wine was served her as she left their bed.
Ramin sat with her, it was he who'd made
The music that awoke her as he played
Sometimes a lute, sometimes a harp, and blent
In song his sweet voice with each instrument,
Singing of love in heart-delighting strains,
Dwelling on love's sweet pleasures and its pains.

Gorgani/Davis

ACKNOWLEDGMENTS

When I started to look for a structure for this book, for which I had been gathering information for quite a few years, I realized that I would first have to convince my editor George Constable that there was such a thing as an Iranian wine drinking tradition. I had to bring to his attention my research into the work of archeologists, linguists, travelers, Persian poets and contemporary scholars who had written about wine and Iran, such as Homa Nateq, Souren Melikian-Chirvani, Willem Floor, Patrick McGovern and Rudi Matthee. If I could convince George, I knew I'd have a book worth pursuing. It was hard, but eventually he accepted that there was more in this book than my usual refrain that everything came from Iran. Thank you George for all your help in structuring the book and helping with the writing, and for bringing to bear your astute and professional attitude to publishing. Without you this would have been a much less worthwhile book.

I would like to thank my sons Zal and Rostam for their often harsh criticisms as well as their aesthetic sensibilities, which forced me to see through their eyes and redouble my efforts to try to get the look of the book right. Thanks are also due to their friends: Hugh MacDonald who helped me in the preliminary stages of this book, Mike and Brit who gave me good suggestions, and Nelly for helping me with research and typing. Thanks also to Chris Eichler at Mage for his close readings of the text, his corrections and his very precise clipping of images.

Many museums provided the art and artifact images included in this book—thank you to all of them. However, I would like to especially thank Massumeh Farhad at the Freer and Sackler Galleries and Mariam Ekhtiar at the Metropolitan Museum for their guidance. Thanks also to Bassam Al-Kahouaji of Bacchus for finding all the wines we needed for the pairings. Special thanks are due to Gordon and Margie Burns, friends and guiding lights of ETS Labs, for both their technical assistance and for providing our team with a second home in St. Helena whenever work on this book took us to the Napa Valley. Many thanks also to Greg Drescher of the Culinary Institute of America at Greystone for his interest in Persian cuisine and for inviting me to teach at their seminars and conferences.

In the kitchen, Greg Diorio, a good cook and future doctor, was a great help both in testing the recipes and in assisting me during the photography—thank you Greg. Thanks also to Lily Warner for her help in typing and testing recipes.

Dick Davis is a friend, a treasure and a godsend for Persian literature in English. Thank you Dick for the many wonderful translations of poems, and the essay on wine and Persian poetry for this book.

Thanks are also due to Burke Owens for his guide to pairing wine with Persian food and for all the great pairings for the recipes—some of your pairings are real taste bud openers.

Thank you to Amir Hossein Tabnak for the beautiful Persian calligraphy of the poems. Thanks also to Afshin Bakhtiari for the photography in Iran and to Bahram Ebrahimi for getting them to us. And, of course, thanks and more are due to my friend and photographer of twenty-five years, Serge Ephraim. Six or seven years ago Serge and I were driving and taking photographs between Samarqand and Bokhara; this year it was between San Francisco and St. Helena with a stop at the Oakville Grocery in between. Finally, I would like to thank my *munés* and life partner Mohammad, who is also my editor-in-chief. I love you always.

Grapes left out to dry in Takistan, near Qazvin, Iran.

INDEX

J. Georges Bondoux 1905

SOURCES & RESOURCES

If you are unable to find local providers for any of the ingredients in the book, the sources below can provide you their products by special delivery. You can also find a regularly updated list of specialty stores at www.mage.com/stores.html.

Darioush Winery
4240 Silverado Trail
Napa, CA 94558
Telephone: 707-257-2345
Fax: 707-257-3132
info@darioush.com • www.darioush.com
Darioush wines can be found at many of the world's finest restaurants and wine merchants, but can be difficult to locate due to their limited production. To purchase wines directly from Darioush, contact the winery concierge and join their 'First Offerings' mail list to receive priority access to all upcoming releases and library offerings. Mail list reservations can be made via phone, email or online

Bacchus Wine Cellar
1635 Wisconsin Avenue, NW
Washington, DC 20007
Telephone: 202-337-2003
bassam@bwcellar.com • www.bwcellar.com
Bassam Al-Kahouaji, my local vintner, is very knowledgeable about wines. Not only does he carry Darioush wines, but his cellar is always active with wine tastings and good cheer.

D'Artagnan
280 Wilson Avenue
Newark, NJ 07150
Telephone: 800-327-8246
orders@dartagnan.com • www.dartagnan.com
Duck, quail, pheasant and many other specialty products are available here.

Dean and Deluca
Telephone: 800-221-7714
www.deananddeluca.com
Verjuice and many other fine foods.

The Date People
P.O. Box 808
Niland, CA 92257
Telephone: 760-359-3211
datefolk@brawleyonline.com
A wonderful source for fresh, organic dates.

Farm 2 Market
P.O. Box 124, Trout Road
Roscoe, NY 12776
Telephone: 800-663-4326
info@farm-2-market.com
www.farm-2-market.com
Suppliers of fresh fish, especially Queens River Sturgeon from the Columbia River Basin near Sacramento, California.

Rockville Gourmet
1331 Rockville Pike
Rockville, MD 20852
301-424-4444
Aqa Reza is the butcher I go to for difficult-to-find meats and cuts such as veal fillet or lamb liver for kebabs.

Soofer Company/Sadaf
2828 S. Alameda St.
Los Angeles, CA 90058
Telephone: 800-852-4050
323-234-2447
info@sadaf.com • www.sadaf.com
Unripe grapes in brine, sun-dried yogurt (kashk) and many other Persian specialty products are all available through their web site.

Vanilla Saffron Imports
949 Valencia Street
San Francisco, CA 94110
Telephone: 415-648-8990
www.saffron.com
A great site for ordering pure sargol, Iranian saffron threads.

A 1905 painting by Jules-George Bondoux of the mound of Susa prior to the start of archeological excavations there.

Wild mustard carpets a vineyard in the Napa Valley in February.